Guest Room Journal
Spring/Summer 2021

edit and design by Andréa Fekete

Copyright 2021
Printed in the United States of America.
Black Crown Books.
An imprint of Guest Room Press.
Charleston, West Virginia/25302
Ingram Distribution.

To place discounted or bulk orders, email
publisher@guestroompress.com

Cover Photo: Taryn Conn
Cover Design: Guest Room Press
ISBN 978-1-735-4277-4-4

All rights reserved. No part of this publication may be reproduced in any manner, distributed or transmitted in any form by any means without prior written permission of the individual contributing authors or artists.
All rights revert to individual authors upon publication.

photo credit: Taryn Conn, Icy Suspension

06. RAJIA HASSIB
What We Remember

17. BILL LYNCH
Sweating out the HeartBreak

19. ANDRÉA FEKETE
When You Can't Control the Pain

23. COOTER RASPUTIN
Barroom Women

26. DOUG VAN GUNDY
Points of Entry

34. KELLI HANSEL HAYWOOD
memoir excerpt from Sacred Catharsis

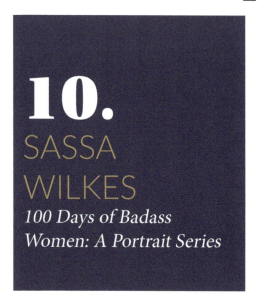

10.
SASSA WILKES
100 Days of Badass Women: A Portrait Series

photo credit: Taryn Conn, Reflective Mud

31. MARIE MANILLA

Fainting Goats memoir excerpt

27. ANN PANCAKE

Alexander Salamander: Letter to my Great-Great Nephew

42. LOOK CLOSER: POETRY

Jodi McMillian, Mary B. Moore, Pauletta Hansel, Ace Boggess, Andréa Fekete

39. LARA LILLIBRIDGE

Running in the Halls

50. INTERVIEWS

Poet Ron Houchin, Retired Major Richard Ojeda II. Chet Lowther, artist

60. ABOUT THE EDITOR

61. TARYN CONN

WEST VIRGINIA PHOTOGRAPHER

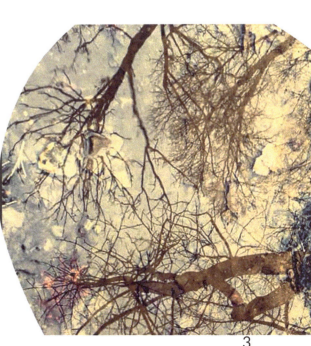

GUEST ROOM JOURNAL
SPRING/SUMMER 2021

Intelligence | Inspiration | Connection | Humor

Look Closer: Mission Statement from the Editor

Guest Room Journal publishes tasteful, intelligent commentary, inspiring personal essays, interviews, humor, photography, art, and high-quality poetry. During a global pandemic, inspiration, rational thought, and connection is needed more than anything. The Guest Room is a space for well-crafted content that's healthy for its readers professionally, emotionally, and intellectually. Guests include new and returning contributors with pieces perpetuating only our best human traits: ingenuity, humor, and resiliency. Social distancing means many rely on "social" media for information and contact, but the current business model of social media perpetuates our worst human tendencies. Those platforms permeate our culture with toxic tribalism, extremism, and misinformation. This journal exists in reaction to that toxicity by returning to a more old-school way of sharing. We can move closer to becoming our best selves, whatever that looks like for each of us in this moment, and creatives can help all of us do that. That's why I decided to start this journal. Guests share universal fears, hopes, and joys unique to no one constructed "category" within which we've confined ourselves. There is more beauty around us than we see, even now in this unprecedented time. I hope these Guests inspire you to slow down, be still, and breathe. I think the world would be a better place if we all looked up from our devices and looked to one another and inside ourselves. I hope you find inspiration here.

BRINGING THE LIGHT: INSPIRING PERSONAL ESSAYS

Rajia Hassib, Sassa Wilkes, Bill Lynch, Andréa Fekete

TELL ME A STORY FROM YOUR LIFE: MEMOIR
Cooter Rasputin, Doug Van Gundy, Kelli Hansel Haywood,
Maria Manilla, Ann Pancake

BECOMING: INTERVIEWS WITH ENGAGING HUMANS
poet Ron Houchin, artist Chet Lowther, Retired Maj. Richard Ojeda

LOOK CLOSER: POETRY
Ace Boggess, Pauletta Hansel, Jodi McMillian, Mary B. Moore, Andréa Fekete

FEATURED PHOTOGRAPHER
Taryn Conn

COVER PAINTING (self-portrait)
Sassa Wilkes

publisher@guestroompress.com | http://guestroompress.com/journal

BRINGING THE LIGHT

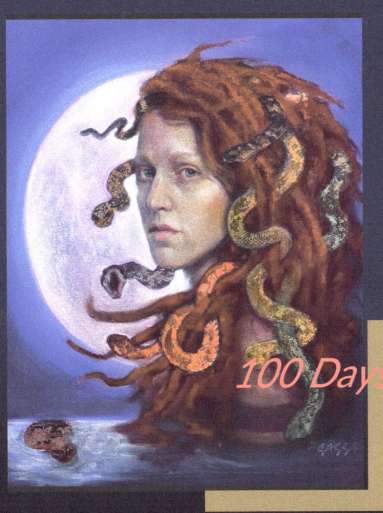

FEATURING

Rajia Hassib
Bill Lynch
Andréa Fekete

100 Days of Badass Women

A Portrait Series
by Sassa Wilkes

WHAT WE REMEMBER — RAJIA HASSIB

When I was in middle school, my family and I moved to a sea-side vacation apartment for the summer and stayed for three years. The apartment was in the beach neighborhood of Al Mamurah, at the edge of the city of Alexandria. A wide promenade and a stretch of manicured gardens separated a row of low apartment buildings from the sandy beach. Beyond that, the neighborhood extended in a grid of streets and wide avenues separating blocks of taller apartment buildings with gardens between them, which gave the area an abundance of greenery unusual in the city. Back then, Alexandria was home to four million inhabitants. The city stretched along the Mediterranean, its main axis defined by the Corniche, the avenue that ran about twenty miles along the sea from downtown Alexandria, where I went to school, to Montazah, the palace of Egypt's former monarch, King Farouk, who used to spend his summers there before he was exiled in 1952. Al Mamurah lay beyond that, at the very eastern tip of what can still be considered the bounds of the city, and the building we lived in sat in the farthest corner of Al Mamurah. Our apartment was the last one on the fourth and highest floor. It was as if we had deliberately chosen to live at the remotest, most isolated corner of the city.

In the summer, Al Mamurah buzzed with vacationers from all over Egypt. During the day, beach goers lounged under colorful umbrellas and snacked on *fresca*—from the Italian word for *fresh*—an assortment of treats vendors peddled in glass boxes carried on one shoulder, clusters of nuts held together with melted sugar and, my favorite, a paper-thin round cookie about eight inches in diameter, made out of two crunchy sheets of pastry glued together with syrup. In the evenings, adults sat on balconies drinking tea and chatting, while teenagers and kids spilled out on the wide sidewalks and promenades, and children riding bikes chased the city trucks dousing the streets in a white cloud of doubtless-carcinogenic anti-mosquito spray. This went on from May till September. Once schools were back in session, the entire neighborhood emptied out and, over the course of a couple of weeks, became almost deserted, with only a handful of Alexandrians choosing to stay on, as my family did.

The apartment we lived in was a perk of my father's job. A retired navy office, my father held a prestigious administrative position in the government, overseeing buildings belonging to the presidential establishment in Alexandria and all along a large section of Egypt's northern coast, including King Farouk's palace nearby, which was now occasionally used to host visiting dignitaries. The presidency also owned a gated community in Al Mamurah, a complex of three large buildings for the use of employees and their families. Our apartment was similar in size to the one I had grown up in, the one we left presumably for a few weeks of vacation and never returned to: two bedrooms, one large living room and dining room combined, one bathroom, and a small kitchen, but it had the added attraction of a nine-foot wide balcony that ran the length of it and overlooked a large garden and, beyond it, the sea. Compared to our own apartment, located in the busy, crowded, loud heart of the city, this one had the advantage of sunlight, privacy, quietness, and a glorious view. For such perks, my parents were willing to put up with the commute, at least until our new apartment, the three-bedroom one we would later move into and which was still under construction, was ready.

I have sporadic but vivid memories of my years in Al Mamurah: sitting on a bed next to an opened window overlooking the sea, listening to Madonna's *True Blue* and playing solitaire (pre-iPhone, using an actual deck of cards); lounging on the white wooden seats with their blue, sea-air moistened cushions out on the balcony and reading; picking fresh grape leaves from a nearby grove with my mother; leaning against the railing of the fourth floor walkway leading to the apartment entrance and watching a parade of cars waving Egypt's flag and honking after Egypt's national soccer team qualified for the World Cup for the first time since 1934; playing squash with my father at a court tucked on the grounds of an abandoned summer cabin that Egypt's former president Nasser had used decades ago and that was only a ten minute walk away, the sound of the black, rubber ball ringing in the court every time it hit one of the tall white walls.

The squash court is where my memory falters. I distinctly remember meeting Mubarak, Egypt's then president, in front of that court. Back then, he was in his fifties, had been in office only a few years, since Sadat was assassinated in 1981, and no one anticipated he would end up ruling the country for thirty years. When I met him, he had just finished playing and was sitting down, surrounded by a group of people, a towel draped around his neck. My father introduced me to him, and Mubarak asked me which school I went to. When I said I went to a German school, he pointed at an overweight man standing nearby and told me to tell him, in German, to eat less pasta. Everyone laughed. I blushed, embarrassed both by the prospect of being rude to the older man and by the fact that, for the moment, I had forgotten the German word for pasta (which, it turns out, is Pasta). I improvised, calling it macaroni (a foreign-sounding pronunciation of the Arabic word for pasta—*macarona*, which, in turn, is derived from the Italian macaroni, or elbow pasta—I cluelessly brought the word full circle*)*. My memory of that exchange is quite vivid. I never forget moments of awkward embarrassment.

Yet I know that this memory cannot have happened the way I recall it. The dates don't add up. Some of my other memories have time stamps: Madonna's *True Blue* was released in 1986, and that soccer match that ensured Egypt's admittance to the World Cup took place on 17 November of 1989, when I was fourteen. Our stay in Al Mamurah had to have taken place between those dates. Yet I know I was much younger when I met Egypt's president—probably nine or ten. I stood in front of a seated Mubarak and was at eye-level with him. We hadn't moved to that apartment in Al Mamurah yet.

A phone call to my father confirms my suspicion: my memory is flawed. I did meet Mubarak, and we did have that exact exchange, only it was another squash court next to a different resort that the military owned, the one in Al Agamy, a beach town twelve miles west of Alexandria, where we vacationed back when my father was an aide-de-camp to the president. That happened five or six years before we moved to Al Mamurah. My father tries to remind me of that other squash court, but I have no memory of the place he describes. The exterior of the court I see Mubarak sitting in front of is the exterior of the court I've entered to play squash with my father so many times. I stand there, in front of a young, laughing Mubarak, and forget the German word for pasta.

~

Memories lie. The particular kind of lie my memory of Mubarak's meeting pulled is called fusion: combining two separate memories into one. Research in psychology assures me that this is quite common, as is our tendency to confabulate, personalize, distort, and contaminate our memories. We are such social creatures that hearing others correct our account of shared events often leads us to revise our own memories of that event, seeing it clearly not as we experienced it but as others tell us we have. People under grueling police investigation can confess to crimes they never committed, fully believing their own confessions. Eyewitness testimony is notoriously unreliable; the Innocence Project, a nonprofit organization working to exonerate the wrongly convicted, claims that 70% of their cases center around false eyewitness testimony. People don't always intentionally lie—they often misremember with firm conviction. Our mind's eye has very poor vision.

~

Now I question all my Al Mamurah memories. Did I really eat *fresca* at that beach, or was that another beach? How come there were so many cars celebrating Egypt's soccer win in November, when the beach neighborhood was doubtless deserted? Did they flock in from other areas, or is my memory inflating two cars into a parade? Did we really have white wooden seats with blue cushions on that balcony, or am I conflating them with the same seats that still stand in the balcony of my parents' current apartment?

If my memories of those three years are so unreliable, doesn't it follow that my future memories of this year will be just as muddled?

~

I try to imagine how I will remember 2020. There is no silver lining to this year, no way to make a year with so much death and sickness seem better than what it is. I ask my husband how he thinks he will remember it. He is an Intensive Care doctor, which has made this year the hardest of his professional career so far. His answer is immediate: *I won't.* He claims that he will suppress the memories of the entire year. He announces this as a plan he fully intends to pursue, which is typical of him—the notion that he can control even how his memory will work. I inform him that my research in psychology shows that suppression has never been scientifically proven, that people's suppressed memories of trauma, once they reemerge, are now widely believed to be fabricated through the processes of therapy, that the debate between psychologists over the validity of suppressed memories was so heated in the 1990s that it was dubbed the "memory wars." But I get what he is saying. No one wants to remember difficult times.

I know there are things about this year that we should never forget: how we collectively failed to protect the most vulnerable among us; how we, as a society, have failed ourselves and how our government has failed us. Even so, and despite knowing that events that illicit a strong emotional response are more deeply carved in our memories, I still indulge in the illusion that I may forget some of the things I've experienced this year. Maybe I will forget the two days my husband spent quarantined in our bedroom as he awaited the test results that confirmed that, despite being exposed to a COVID-19 positive patient, he hadn't contracted the virus. Maybe I will forget sitting with him, going over our finances to make sure I'd be able to afford mortgage payment and college tuition for our kids if he were to die. Maybe I will forget how he drafted his will and how we both sent it to his cousin, ensuring that he would act as executor in case my husband got sick and infected me and we both died. Maybe I will forget his frustration at people calling the disease he has treated and seen people die of a hoax. Maybe I will forget the anger of knowing that, nine months into the pandemic, he and his coworkers still have to ration their protective gear. Maybe I will forget the time he and I spent researching the maximum hours a disposable N95 mask—the one he is supposed to throw away after each patient encounter—can be reused before it loses effectiveness, whether he can safely stretch each mask's use for a week. Maybe I will forget the name N95. Maybe, one day, he and I will be sitting on our family room sofa, watching old Vincent Price horror movies for the umpteenth time, and I will turn to him and ask: what was the name of that mask we were so desperate to find during the pandemic? Maybe my memory will be so flawed that it will rename the mask to something totally irrelevant. Maybe I will believe it was called the M85, which is the name of both a machine gun and a galaxy 60 million lightyears away.

~

I have only minimal care for historical accuracy. I will leave the task of documenting this year as it happened to historians and will leave the concern about the accuracy of recalled events to memoirists. As a fiction writer, I find the prospect of false memories alarmingly exciting—maybe I will get to make up my own past and believe it, too. In a way, fiction writers make a profession out of what we all often do when we remember: tell a story that never happened with supreme conviction.

Al Mamurah was thirty years ago, but research proves that memories get distorted and contaminated much faster. We start forgetting events a mere twenty minutes after they happen. A study conducted in 1981 showed that eyewitness identification was accurate after three days but 35% false after five months. The longer the time, the more our memories lose their accuracy. The more we are likely to make things up and believe they truly happened.

In a few years, I may have a significantly fictionalized memory of 2020. If I were to talk about this year with friends and family, we would doubtless all contribute our respective faulty recollections, creating a collaborative, unreliable narrative. I find this quite alluring, even soothing, partly because it blurs the line between fiction and reality, but mostly because it implies survival. We can recall bad times only if we lived through them and made it, scathed but alive, to the other side. So what if what we recall is deeply flawed? All what matters is this: one day, hopefully, we will be able to turn to a loved one and ask: Do you remember? Do you remember what we lived through together? Do you remember?

Rajia Hassib was born and raised in Alexandria, Egypt, before moving to the US at age twenty-three. A decade later, she returned to college to study English Writing and Literature and to pursue her life-long dream of becoming a writer. She holds a BA and an MA in English, both from Marshall University. After graduation, she worked briefly as a part-time Instructor of English at Marshall University, teaching an Introduction to Creative Writing class as well as a class on Postcolonial Literature. She lives in Charleston, WV with her husband and two children. You can find her at rajiahassib.com

Turning on the Light
Sassa Wilkes

Inspiration isn't looking for me. It has no interest in seeking me out, and it never has. I know it's true, yet I still slide back into the comfort of the lie. I'm waiting. I'm trying to think of an idea. I'm looking for inspiration. That last one is juicy, isn't it? *Looking. Searching. Seeking.* What heroic verbs! It never works. Inspiration isn't looking for me, and it won't come when it's called, either. It's kind of like an asshole cat.

I have only ever experienced genuine inspiration in the doing. Which sucks, because doing is the hardest thing when I feel uninspired. When uninspired turns into depression, doing anything at all is damn near impossible. You can relate, yes? 2020 is such a hag.

Toward the end of last year, I really got my stuff together. I used all the planning skills I've learned from procrastination, planning, and mapped out a pretty boss 2020. I projected twelve months of classes, private lessons, and events at my studio. I factored in time for personal, meaningful art making. Everything was color coded. Success was imminent. My wall calendar looked like a giant vanilla cake with post-it sprinkles, and I cut myself a huge congratulatory slice. The Universe, in its infinite wisdom, taught me a lesson by poisoning the hell out of it with COVID-19.

I'm good in a crisis. COVID struck, my husband was laid off, and my classes were cancelled. I got creative and came up with some ways to make money and help. I did tiny watercolor commissions. I assembled a group of creative people, did a month-long art swap by mail, and saw endless examples of resilience and adaptability. Zoom was the hip new bar. Local shops transitioned to selling online with live auctions. Armies of seamsters cranked out masks that didn't even hurt your ears. The entire country of Italy

hung out on their balconies all day and sang in perfect harmony. Companies that used to sell party supplies began manufacturing inspirational memes. The internet became the real world, and the world was seemingly full of inspiration. For me, this COVID comradery lost its flavor with alarming quickness. I shouldn't have been surprised. It was a dish made with dangerous ingredients. The combination of cabin fever, increased internet connection, anxiety-provoking news, and heartfelt blog posts served up a dizzying cognitive dissonance.

Self-preservation unplugged me and dragged me outside. The earth had warmed up, and it felt good under my bare feet. I gathered all the fallen tree limbs I could find. I built a fence along the woods. I started the garden I've always wanted, using the largest limbs for a tomato teepee. I learned about German Hügelkultur, and constructed a huge organic spiral out of wood, grass trimmings, food waste, and I planted herbs in it. My back yard looked like Mother Nature

> "THIS HAS BEEN THE DARKEST YEAR I CAN REMEMBER, AND I'M TURNING ON THE LIGHTS."

and the Blair Witch got wine-drunk and had a fort-making contest. I was getting plenty of exercise, vitamin D, and fresh, organic food. Too bad the bills were piling up. Too bad I couldn't pay them with vegetables.

I wrapped up my gardening season without a plan for what was next. I spent weeks in a disorienting fog, anxious and seriously depressed. Election season cranked into high gear, plopping a turd-cherry on my garbage sundae. People were dropping like flies, but at least we still had Ruth Bader Ginsberg.

The death of RBG made me sad as hell, although I wasn't terribly knowledgeable about her life. I think I felt the sadness of the collective, this group that was growing increasingly fearful of the election results. It broke me, and I soothed myself with painting.

Painting is good for me. It's good for me in the way that exercise and nutritious food are good for me, so naturally I sometimes avoid it. Depression makes all those good things easier to avoid, doesn't it?

Wanting to honor and learn about the life of Ruth brought me back to my easel, and it felt really, really good to paint. Under normal circumstances, I may not have shown anyone that painting. I would not have shared all my squishy feelings about it like I did. But quarantine had gone on so long at this point that even introverts were starting to miss hugs, and I was raw. I shared the painting and spilled all my internal beans quite publicly, and the response to it was so warm; it felt just like a big hug. I spent a few days after that deciding what to do next; I compared the darkness I was trying to climb out of to the challenge someone faces trying to lose weight. It's smart to eliminate junk food from the house. It's smart to work out with a buddy for accountability. It's smart to make goals, to surround yourself with positive encouragement. I dusted off my stupid wall calendar and tore off all the post-it sprinkled pages to see what was left of the year, and I made a plan. I published a promise on my website and shared it everywhere, so I wouldn't back out. The heading of my site's new homepage read: As of September 23, there are 100 days left in 2020. This has been the darkest year I can remember, and am turning on the lights.

Every day for the next 100 days, I'm going to paint and learn about a woman who inspires me and share it here. My second painting was of Maya Angelou. I set my iPad up beside my easel, and listened to interviews with her the entire time I painted. I've done this for every painting. A few times I've felt tempted to listen to music or play some other movie, but I just can't; it doesn't work.

Listening to my subjects speak and learning about their lives comes through the paint in a way I can't describe, and I don't want to fake it. I didn't anticipate getting so immersed in the writing I would do, but it was hard not to share my thoughts. In many cases, what I learned each day and how I felt after painting felt more important to share than the paintings themselves. I also did not anticipate the response that this project would have from the people following it. I begangetting piles of messages with recommendations of women to paint. News stations started calling me for interviews.

The concept of inspiration suddenly felt ever-present to me. People described the work I was doing and the women I was painting as inspiring. News stations and articles used that term to avoid saying what I've alw called thiscalled this project; 100 Badass Women. I felt inspired, truly, and I didn't want to lose that feeling. I've had a lot of time at my easel to think about what it really means and where it comes from. I created this project to give myself what I felt I needed, and the motivation to see it through. In a sense, I was trying to create a perfect environment for inspiration to live. I knew it wasn't looking for me, and I knew I couldn't command it. But what if I just sat out all its favorite treats and left my door open? "I had to listen to the words of wise, accomplished, and fierce women all day, every day, for the rest of this godforsaken year." And in many ways, it has really worked. The promise I made to people following my work has led me dutifully to my easel every day. And the act of learning about the positive impact of women throughout history has certainly been enlightening. I do feel inspired, but I realized recently that I don't think it's coming from where I expected it to. recently that I don't think it's coming from where I expected it to.

I get many messages a day from people sharing their memories of my subjects, their feelings about the work, or nominating a new woman for me to paint. Several have been from men who privately messaged me nominations to paint their mothers, with paragraphs of reasons she is a badass in their eyes. I've gotten the most encouraging mail from followers. I've been the recipient of emotional support, and downright Appalachian kindness I didn't know I needed. A friend from school delivered homemade meals to my family to help me keep painting. I've had so many good conversations about women, power, politics, and passion. I've made new friends that I can't wait to hang out with in real life. It took me seventy-nine paintings to realize that the inspiration to keep painting and to remain positive is coming not from the women I paint, but from the people with whom I'm sharing my work.

I absolutely love learning about these women. I'm fascinated by and enjoy sharing their stories with others. Now I understand that the work itself is the language I'm using to communicate, to feel fully seen, and allow others to feel seen in their responses. It's the only language I have that can create that feeling for me. This project feels like a total immersion in that language; I'm starting to sense a fluency. Inspiration wasn't looking for me. Far from it. It didn't come when it was called. It only showed up when I showed up first; let go and got lost in the doing even without it there to help me. When it finally came around, it revealed its truth to me one brushstroke at a time.

photo credit: Sassa Wilkes, self

BIO (from iamsassa.com)

"I am a 39 year old teacher, mother, and compulsive art-maker. Art is the language I use to communicate and connect with others. I don't ever really feel that my work is complete until it's been shared, and I love the conversations it can spark. I have gained such valuable insight and wisdom from this kind of community sharing that most of my work feels collaborative in a sense.

The things I make can vary wildly.
I am forever in love with oil paint, but I enjoy using a huge variety of other media to express my ideas. Thank you from the bottom of my heart for all of your love and support of my work. I am so grateful to be able to do what I love and share it with others."

The following three paintings are by Sassa. Meryl Streep, Judy Garland, and Vice President Kamala Harris.

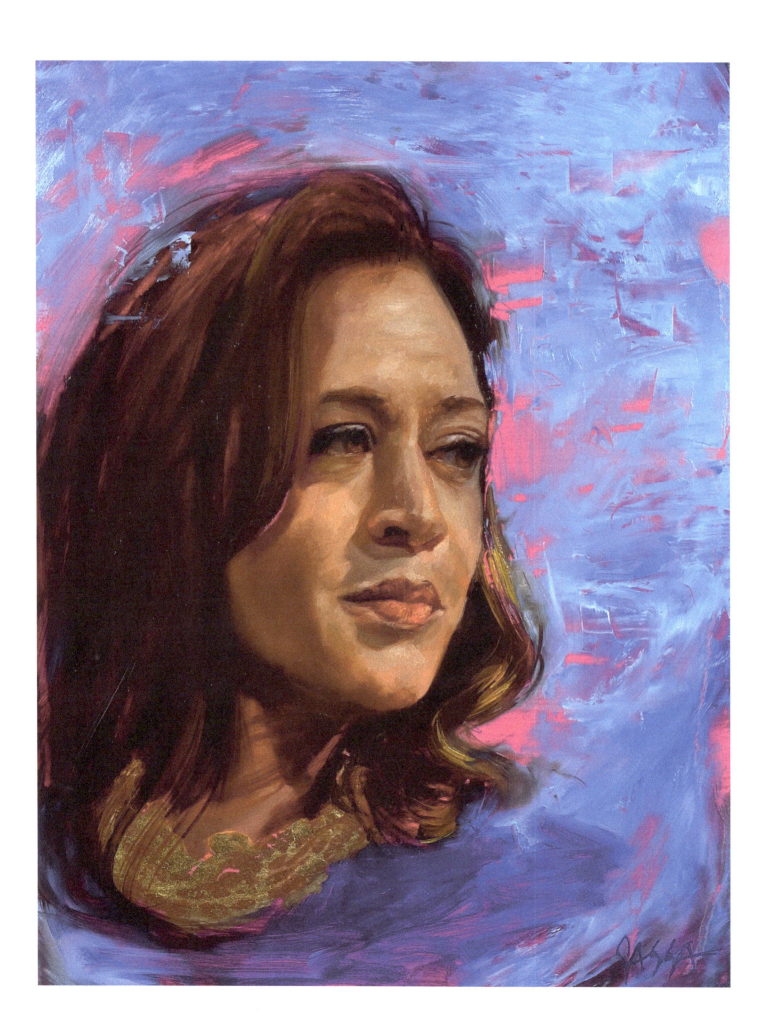

BILL LYNCH

SWEATING OUT HEARTBREAK: MAKING SPACE FOR HEALING

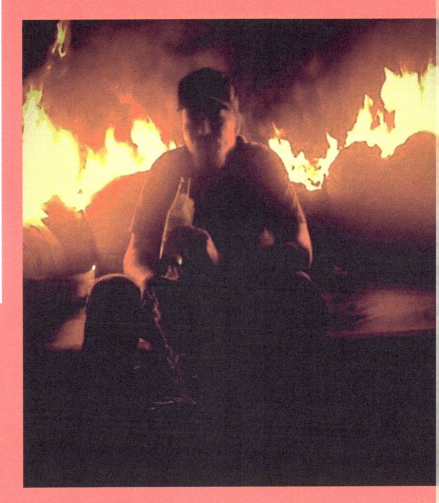

photo credit: Taryn Conn

A teenage girl, slender and as lithe as a deer, flies past me, on the left. Her blond, braided hair trails behind, struggling to keep up. I look down as she passes, past her narrow shoulders and tiny waist, past even her jet-black leggings which accentuate her fit body.

I look to her feet and try to figure out what's she's doing that I'm not and why, even though I'm clearly a head taller, she runs so much faster, so effortlessly. Why can't I be graceful, too? How is it she can pass me? Why can't I keep up? I hate to run –or I don't. I can't make up my mind most days, but four or five times a week I strap on my worn and ragged running shoes, find a playlist on my phone, and then take off down the road.

I will grumble that I ought to quit for the first half mile, make excuses in my head about my knees, how it feels wrong, before I finally give up and decide that I'm just going to do this even if I'm not very good, even if I'm not very fast.

I'm going to do this because I need to do this. Running is part of what has kept me functional, not frantic, in one of the hardest years of my life. I'm not saying I'm anything special.

We've all had a hard year with the pandemic. In the past 12 months, most of us have, in the famous words of Thoreau, "lived lives of quiet desperation." We've stayed away from friends and family, kept to ourselves like hermits or prisoners, watched more television than any of us could have ever wanted while we hoped this plague would pass our doors. Almost all of us know somebody who wasn't so lucky: an old high school buddy, the father of a coworker, a woman from church.

I came back to running after a long break away from it. I ran in high school, in 10th grade, but then later discovered cigarettes and beer and had to give it up. After several decades of predictably bad choices, I reached a terrible, awful physical state. By 49, I'd ballooned up to 265 pounds and had developed high blood pressure that turned into essential hypertension.

Most of this I put off to the unavoidable entrenchment of middle age. My cholesterol numbers were also bad, but then things began to go wrong with my kidneys and terrified, I put myself on a diet.

After a few months and some success, I began attending group fitness classes in a repurposed industrial building located beside a set of railroad tracks

17

and perpetually downwind of the cedar mulch pile at the garden center next door. Between the diet and the exercise, I lost about 85 pounds and came to have a better understanding of not just my body, but also how my head worked. I'm a worrier, have been my whole life. My family doctor warned me about that when I was 14 and being treated for severe acne. I was an anxious kid and Dr. McGuire thought the anxiety had something to do with my blossoming acne… and my insomnia… and probably the stammer. "It's good to have people who are concerned about things," she said. "But it's hard to do that all the time." She prescribed pills and lotion for my face, but I self-medicated with whatever was in the kitchen for the rest. Food soothed me and as I went from being an anxious teenager to a frequently stressed adult, the pounds crept on naturally, but really began to get out of hand in my 40s. My personal history sounds like a great television sitcom but is harder in practice. I work for a newspaper, not exactly the best paying or most stable occupation. I'm a twice-divorced single dad and a reluctant homeowner. While I pretended to be a gym rat and maintained a monthly subscription to the local YMCA, my most regular exercise came from lifting weighted spoons and forks to my mouth. It was the most reliable stress relief I had and safer than drinking. I clearly had a problem. After I had my little "come to Jesus" moment with my health, I confronted not just what I ate, but also why I ate. Feasting was a copy mechanism, a way to create temporary equilibrium when everything felt like chaos, but everything always felt like chaos all the time. My job didn't seem stable. Home was drudgery and resentment. My fiancé told me she loved me, but wouldn't set a date.

Regular, routine exercise was my answer, a reliable way to release stress, while also taking a break from whatever evil chipmunk of a thought was burowing through my brain. This is the chief reason I like CrossFit. The jumping, lifting and hauling-ass that's part of every workout is awful. After almost every class, we joke about how none of us liked doing whatever we just did. Yet, we all show up the next day. We keep showing up. CrossFit is brilliant in that while you're in the middle of workout, you would be hard-pressed to think about anything besides what you are doing at that very moment. You're too busy pressing weights over your head or diving to the floor to do a burpee to have a rational thought besides, "Oof. This is hard." Running is the opposite, but also effective. When I start running, I'm entirely in my head, mulling over a laundry list of complaints, objections and outrages. I think about my every unhappiness. I think about my failings. I seethe. I burn. I break apart, but I keep running.

By the third mile, I've let it all go. By the time I walk to my car, my burdens are lighter, and I really just want a snack and maybe a shower. Maintaining the discipline of getting up, getting to the gym or going out to run has changed my life. I'm stronger and healthier than I was when I was half my age. I feel better, which I think makes me more patient and more even tempered. I still worry about all kinds of things, but the worries don't swallow me up as much as they used to. It's easier to shrug off little annoyances and just be kind. Exercise probably saved my life. My fiancé, who couldn't commit to a wedding date, dumped me in a parking lot. There'd been someone else for a while.

A year later, they were married. Having miles to run and weights to lift helped me sweat out some of that heartbreak. It made space in my head so that when I I wasn't running, I could think about forgiveness, mercy and even gratitude for the time we'd had. I cannot fathom how much ice cream I'd have had to eat or how much beer I'd have had to drink to numb myself to that particular pain.

Then, in the early Spring of 2020, I was laid off from my job at the paper. The pandemic forced management into a corner. I was a regrettable budget cut. The thing I'd feared so long had finally come to pass, but running every morning, sometimes 10 miles at a time, helped me find my bearings. I was OK. I was better than OK. I was resilient. Even after the newspaper brought me back, I kept running. I kept moving. I was strong. I could not control what the rest of the world did, but I could control what I did, and I chose to put one foot in front of another and just keep going.

WHEN YOU CAN'T CONTROL THE PAIN: PRO TIPS

BY ANDRÉA FEKETE

photo credit: Taryn Conn

Why did I feel just a little prepared for the insane amount of misery we'd all share in 2020? Because I've been in physical pain since 2009. For years, I struggled with an undiagnosed illness because my specialist dismissed my complaints. I had endometriosis and thoracic outlet syndrome.

Because my doctor dismissed my complaints, like doctors often dismiss women's complaints, I had to go on what felt like the Official World Tour of Doctors. It wasn't their specialty, so of course, they missed the diagnosis, too. Yay. I wasn't living with occassional pain, or moderate pain, but years of constant, untreated severe pain. I had poor quality of life, destroyed plans, and more isolation than I'd ever experienced. I still have pain, but not at that level and not due to that disease.

The only experience I can compare to years of undiagnosed, untreated pain is living in the isolating, high-stress era of the COVID-19 pandemic, although I felt a little more prepared than most for tolerating impressive amounts of utter bullshit. Pandemic isolation is similar to my life before diagnosis. I self-isoalted I didn't want to be around others, trying to make normal conversation when all I could think about was the pain. The pain, which was at a good, strong 8 on the pain scale each day (except on the worst days when it was a 10) was only one of the myriad of symptoms I tolerated. I could do almost nothing that wasn't impacted or downright ruined by the illness and its side effects. Before I had treatment, there was one word in my mind upon waking and one before sleep: pain.

In WV, you're almost never given opioids because of the doctors who got everyone addicted years ago.. The opioid crisis means you're going to be denied much in the way of pain relief. Congratulations. What to do? (besides cry or jump off the nearest bridge) I used to jog on days I experienced the most agony. Jogging doesn't help at first. It doesn't "help" the pain at all, actually. It controls to what extent you mind being in pain, and sometimes, that's as good as it gets. I can control where I put my focus, that's it.

> "You can enjoy the moment or not enjoy the moment, but you do not have to be *bound* by it." —Deepak Chopra

We can't control the pandemic, but we can control our response. I'm choosing to listen to stories that inspire me. I'm choosing to focus, to try a little more each day to heal the unhealed in myself, and to offer comfort to others where I can. We're all in pain now. Not one person who believes the virus is a real threat isn't in pain. When I jogged, I focused on the heat on my face, my breathing, and the breeze which seemed to carry me from the pain for a little while.

The most profound thing anyone has said to me regarding pain was a friend with spina bifida. Like me, he lived in constant pain. He said, "The question isn't *are you in pain*? The question is, do you *mind* being in pain? It's the minding that's the problem." He had ways of coping that worked for him, mostly ways that helped him manage the *minding*. He smokes weed and indulges in meaningful hobbies. That pretty much explains this pandemic. All we can do is manage the minding of the pain.

I'm not going to feed you some toxic lies about how you could treat this as an opportunity for growth, or how you can push through, and how this will only make you a badass, except that's exactly what I'm saying. I'm allowed because that thinking is exactly why I'm still here. I'm saying this is how I'm coping, and maybe try it on, see if it fits. If not, kick it to the back of the closet, but what if it does fit? What if my friend's ideas about minding pain saves you? This allowing of pain. This sitting with it.

> 66
> "WE CAN'T CHOOSE TO VANISH THE DARK, BUT WE CAN CHOOSE TO KINDLE THE LIGHT." —EDITH EGER, HOLOCAUST SURVIVOR, AUTHOR OF *THE CHOICE*

Sometimes pain and destruction is necessary in creation, such as in nature. Tectonic plates shift to force the ground into mountains. Water cuts rock creating canyons. In the absence of humans, trees slowly shoot through concrete and pull down buildings occupying their space. Like the earth, humans change tremendously during upheaval. This change takes place on its own, often during periods of great suffering. Your body possesses amazing intelligences, running countless processes without conscious interference from you: breathing, renewing cells, digestion, sweating, healing, growing a fetus. Your mind and body, however damaged or imperfect, is built for self-preservation, to even heal its own broken bones. Your brain offers you a shot of adrenaline when under attack, endorphins when you exercise, and oxytocin for falling in love. Emotional pain has its purpose, too. Your body speaks to you in the form of hormones but also "gut feelings." You are of nature and like nature, you are built to know, to heal, to change. So, allow it to hurt. Listen to the alarm, sit with it, ask what it needs. Let the foundation rock. Let it split open. Each break will naturally calcify over stronger than before, like pouring gold in the cracks of a broken teacup, like healed bones, as hard as the ground under your feet.

Making this journal took way too long. I can't type longer than a few minutes. Can't drive longer than half an hour, not without agony. A week before my first of 2 surgeries at the Cleveland Clinic, I'm finally finishing up. Nothing matters more to me than channeling my pain into something greater than myself. I encourage all of you to channel pain. If today isn't that day, then rest without guilt. We all deserve compassion, especially from ourselves. As for me? I'm now writing a memoir about being a chronic patient for a decade, a journey that will come to an end soon I hope. I'm grateful to have made this journal right before I step into the unknown conclusion of my pain story.

> "Like the Gita says, the realest part of you water cannot wet. Wind cannot dry. Weapons cannot shatter. Fire cannot burn. Because it is ancient. It is unborn. It never dies."
> —Deepak Chopra

Pictured: Andréa Fekete
Rafaél Barker Photography 2019

TELL ME A STORY FROM YOUR LIFE

memoir

FEATURING

Doug Van Gundy
Ann Pancake
Kelli Hansel Haywood
Lara Lillibridge
Marie Manilla
Cooter Rasputin

BARROOM WOMEN

by Most Exalted aka Cooter Rasputin

I was at my Aunt's bar the other day. I've been going there since I was a little kid (been in bars since I was about 3 years old). Now when I climb up on a stool my aunt slides a Miller Lite across the bar to me instead of a can of soda. I still remember the day she said to me, "It's so strange to see you standing there like Brother (what she called my Dad) and now you're drinking a beer too." It was like a mile marker that saw me go from childhood straight towards middle age all in a single sentence.

I decided to stop in because Aunt Phyllis is going to close the bar within the year and, like people say, that will be that. Her bar has been a place of such unchanging constancy. The only thing that lets you know what era you're in is what kind of TV is on the wall and what the beer mirrors look like. I can still see the dent in the bar where my Uncle Charlie slapped the end of a sawn off baseball bat down on it to squash whatever tempers were flaring. The biggest change now is there's a wall full of photographs of all the friends and family members I had among the patrons there who are dead now.

My father and two uncles are there. While we were sitting at the bar, I asked Aunt Phyllis if she had heard what it was that killed my other aunt, her baby sister. "I believe it was an aneurysm," my cousin Billy said, from the end of the bar. I was sad thinking of her being gone, but grateful that it wasn't related to dope. She had been fighting that for so long, it felt like a small win that she left the planet without having succumbed to her addiction. It was the last little victory she could get, but it was hard won, and I raised my beer to her memory before finishing the rest of the can.

Another cousin of mine was sitting at the bar. Her mother had died the night before. The weight of it was visible in the way she sat and the look in her eyes, but she had seen it coming; she was ready. She'd devoted the last few years of her life to making sure her mother was taken care of. I've always loved my cousin Dutch; she was a presence full of smiles and kindness throughout my childhood but seeing her willingness to take the emotional beating you receive when you usher a loved one through their convalescence into death made me proud. From my Dad's place at the corner of the bar, I learned over and hugged her and kissed the side of her head and told her I loved her. Even when it feels like there's so much more to say, that has been the way it's handled at my aunt's bar for as long as I've been around, and everyone understands what's implicit when we embrace because they feel it, too.

We talked about death and everyone who was gone, what they meant to us. We understood the gravity of our loss but spoke as if they had just stepped out the door at last call. I thought of how some say there's a certain form of immortality when people remember you after you've died. If that's the case, many who have passed through the door at that tiny bar will live forever or at least, for as long as I'm alive, and now, for as long as you're alive, too.

RASPUTIN......page 2

I promise carrying their ghosts won't be so heavy you'll even notice them there. They might only exist a a tickle somewhere in your brain when you notice the scars in a bar-top, or when you watch the smoke drifting off a cigarette.

Conversation flowed for a while between slow sips on beer and I mentioned a mentor and friend of mine who had died a few years before, "She was an Eastern Kentucky dyke with a master's degree in Journalism, a descendent of Russian Jews, and her father was well known for being a clown -- she sounds like a character from a book and lived like one too. She got me drunk for the first time when I was 19 years old and I worked for her selling cameras in the mall. I loved her dearly." There were smiles and laughs when I used my mentor's own words to describe her as I told her story like so many stories I had heard told there before. We could laugh because when I described her it was like she had only just stepped outside the door. When I was finished, I could see my family members and the bar patrons carrying her ghost and the imperceptible way they tipped their beer to her as they took another sip.

photo credit: Cooter Rasputin

photo credit: Cooter Rasputin, self-portrait

Cooter Rasputin is a photographer from West Virginia. Formal portraits and planned images have long been a part of how he works, but he has also created work in less controlled settings with a documentary style that owes much to his experience with portraiture, darkroom work, and past experiences handling film in a photo lab. His goal has always been to push himself to create new work and expand the boundaries of his own abilities. A sampling of his images are located at www.mostexalted.com and some of his writing is available there in his newsletter archive.

POINTS OF ENTRY

by Doug Van Gundy

I. I fall headlong into a three-foot deep pool in an oxbow of a small stream while trout fishing with my father in the Unita mountains of Utah. I am five years old. The pool is patterned with sunlight and the swift current forces me into the cut bank beneath a huge cottonwood tree. The sun through the bubbles and turbulent water is blue and green and white, and so surprising and beautiful that it doesn't occur to me to be afraid. My father is suddenly beside me and hoisting me back into the air by the placket of my shirt. Only when I see his face, deep behind his beard, twisted into a wordless grimace, do I cry out.

II. My great aunt Justine never buys me anything but books. For birthdays, for Christmas, for no particular reason at all, she buys me books. She is sixty-six years my senior, and an English professor and my hero. She indulges my every intellectual enthusiasm and I still have the books that she bought me on mummification, paper airplanes and Native American mythology. When we are both older, she gives me her pencil-annotated personal copies of Virginia Woolf and James Joyce and Bernard Malamud. Her copy of Life Along the Passaic River has William Carlos Williams' autograph taped to the flyleaf.

III. Mine was a junior high school where the lines of class warfare were clearly drawn: if you had money, you were a Jock – whether or not you played sports; if you didn't have money, you were a Redneck, and there was no question if you hunted, or if your family owned a truck, because you did and they did. I didn't hunt or play sports or have money. My mother was an ER nurse, my father was a Biology professor, and I was way more interested in music and books than guns and cars. Socially, I was fucked.

IV. One summer, while visiting with my Aunt Justine in San Francisco, I left my paperback copy of The Snows of Kilimanjaro and Other Stories on the coffee table in her living room. She picked it up by one corner and asked disdainfully, "Are you reading this?" When I admitted that I was, she told me that she had known Hemmingway a little during the summer of 1924 when she lived in Paris after graduate school. "Ernie", she told the seventeen-year-old me, "was an asshole."

V. When I encountered the poems of James Wright in an Intro to Creative Writing class at the University of Utah, I was thunderstruck. I was sitting on a sofa in the student union with the doorstop of The Norton Anthology bent open across my knee, when I first read "Northern Pike". While the biographical note called Wright, "Midwestern", I knew that was dead wrong. He was as Appalachian as me. Until that moment, I didn't know that you could make art out of cattails and muskrats and crawdads (even if they required an explanatory footnote), or that a life anything like mine could be worthy of poetry. "There must be something very beautiful in my body,/I am so happy."

VI. I have a remarkably sticky brain. Lines of dialog, stanzas of poems, the melodies of songs – they all get stuck in my head like moths on flypaper. Once, I had "The Spanish Flea" by Herb Alpert and the Tijuana Brass on repeat in the jukebox of my skull for fourteen months.
Fourteen.
Months.

VII. In an attempt to fulfill the obligation that came with the gift of an old violin, I asked around for someone to help me learn a tune or two – "Twinkle Twinkle", "Three Blind Mice" – anything. A friend directed me to Mose Coffman. Mose was born in 1905 and learned to play the fiddle before he had ever heard a radio. The man who taught him to fiddle was a Civil War veteran; the woman who taught him the banjo was a freed slave. Almost every Wednesday for over a year, I visited him in the nursing home where he lived. Whenever I would scratch out anything even remotely resembling the tune he'd played for me, he'd tilt his head in my direction and say, "You can't learn this music all in one day."

VIII. In graduate school, Nora Mitchell suggested that I might like the poems of Eamon Grennan. In his work I found so much of what I love in poetry: ekphrasis, nature, kindness, bewilderment, and music. Grennan's poems are as lyrical as any out there, and the boldness with which he pursues the music in a line emboldened me. When I met him years later, I was surprised to discover that he himself is not a musician. Given the ear that he brings to the page, I had just assumed.

IX. In one of my classes this semester, a student blushed and shook her head when I praised a particularly wonderful essay that she had written. "Whenever I write something that I think might be good, I'm afraid that it might be the last good thing I ever write," she said. Shouldn't there be a badge or a sash or a medallion we can present to people like her whenever they finally recognize that they belong to our tribe?

Doug Van Gundy directs the MFA writing program at West Virginia Wesleyan College. His poems, essays and reviews have appeared in many national and international publications, including *Poetry, The Guardian,* and *The Oxford American*. He is co-editor of the anthology *Eyes Glowing at the Edge of the Woods: Contemporary Writing from West Virginia* and author of a collection of poems, *A Life Above Water*, published by Red Hen Press. Doug is also a master traditional fiddler, and plays fiddle, guitar, mandolin, and harmonica in the old-time string duo, Born Old. He has won many awards for his fiddle and banjo playing.

ANN PANCAKE

Alexander Salamander:
Letter to my Great-Great Nephew

photo credit: Taryn Conn. Titled, "Eyes Never Opened to the World"

Dear Alexander,

Your face came to me the other day as I was walking the rail trail above the mine drainage pond not far from my Preston County home. This was after another heavy rain during that spring of endless rain, and there I was, not a quarter mile from that orange treatment pond, when I looked down and spied a salamander crossing the trail. They say salmanders are one of those beings can't survive what we've done to our places, a sensitive species, a coalmine canary. And it was true; I hadn't seen more than a handful of salamanders in the 50 years since I was your age, Alexander, six years old and playing in the creek behind our Nicholas County house. I saw plenty of them then. That's why I think of you, a hundred years from now, playing in your own West Virginia creek. Alexander. Salamander.

    Your great-grandfather, my nephew Jack, was the first generation of our family to be born outside West Virginia since we migrated in from Europe in the 1700's. Jack's mother, my sister, like so many of us West Virginians, left, for work, for health, to raise her kids away from the kinds of ruin here. I remember 2006, when your great-grandfather was four years old and visiting West Virginia from California. I half-carried him, half-walked and -waded him, way up Mill Creek, pointing out sunfish and stocked trout. But certainly, never a salamander. At the end of the day, we had to bathe him, like we had to do after swimming when I was a kid. The ear infections we used to get, the boils on our legs.

    But after 2020, the whole country upended. You'll learn that history soon if you don't know it yet. By the time Jack's son, your grandfather, finished school in 2050, West Virginia was a better place to make a life than California was. You see, what happened here first eventually happened everywhere else. And because we had so much practice with things falling apart, West Virginians, through it all, held onto their best qualities: decency, integrity, kindness, generosity. So, you, Alexander, have known nothing but this place. Your salamanders. Your 2120 West Virginia creek.

    Back on that rainy May day in 2020, after I marveled at the first salamander, I saw a second one. Not deformed, not struggling, both of them perfect. Both of them that beautiful spotted red-orange. And how in God's name were two salamanders squiggling across a former rail bed on the edge of six square miles of abandoned mines? Mines draining their acid into that poison ochre lake?

    Alexander, I think I know.

    Something we learned that same hard spring, while we were bunkered in against the virus, and it snowed on Mother's Day weekend. The temperatures plunged into record-breaker 20s for four nights in a row. Every single tiny newborn leaf on many, many trees—poplar, sycamore, walnut, sassafras, oak—froze black. And the grief we felt, the horror even, that year of many horrors. And what we learned when, over the next four weeks, almost every one of those trees rested a bit. Took a breath. And made thousands of brand

(PANCAKE.....page 2)

new leaves. There you are, Alexander, spending all afternoon in your creek, not a machine in sound or sight. Your people, yes, collaborate with machines, but with discerning wisdom now. That's one of dozens of ways things shifted; that's one of dozens of reasons your water is clean. Your father and grandfather, like others of their generations, learned how to be men without the illusion that a machine could extend the power of their bodies, without the fantasy that a machine could expand the power of their minds. Woke up and understood that real power will always eventually vanquish false power.

You come to terms with that, or all terms are up.

Which led to you, Alexander, your health, your vibrancy, your joy, your clear creek and your salamanders. And if you're thirsty, you don't run back to the house to gulp from a plastic bottle. When you get thirsty, Alexander, you kneel. You brace your palms on the bank. You lean forward, drop your chest. You close your eyes, sink the bottom of your face into the creek, make an "oh" with your lips. And you drink.

Ann Pancake's second short story collection, *Me and My Daddy Listen to Bob Marley,* was published by Counterpoint Press in February 2015. Her first novel, *Strange As This Weather Has Been* (Counterpoint 2007), features a southern West Virginia family devastated by mountaintop removal mining. Based on interviews and real events, the novel was one of Kirkus Review's Top Ten Fiction Books of 2007, won the 2007 Weatherford Award, and was a finalist for the 2008 Orion Book Award. Pancake's first collection of short stories, *Given Ground,* won the 2000 Bakeless award, and she has also received a Whiting Award, an NEA Grant, a Pushcart Prize, and creative writing fellowships from the states of Washington, West Virginia, and Pennsylvania. Her fiction and essays have appeared in journals and anthologies like The Georgia Review, Poets and Writers, Narrative, and New Stories from the South. She earned her BA in English at West Virginia University and a PhD. in English Literature from the University of Washington. She taught in the low-residence writing program at Pacific Lutheran University from 2003 - 2017 and now teaches Appalachian fiction at West Virginia University. She lives near Morgantown in a small rural town with big stories.

FAINTING GOATS BY MARIE MANILLA

We used to faint on purpose, Cher, Dee Dee, and I. Before we started smoking pot and robbing our parents' liquor cabinets, we'd race to the woods behind my house and practice the art of hyperventilation. Quick, deep inhales until we'd hold our breath and one of us would squeeze the other from behind, lift us off our feet, then gently lay us on the ground after we passed out. The last time I did it, a starry sky filled my head. I reached for those flickering lights and was still grasping, arms raised, when sunlight slid beneath my eyelids and pulled me awake. We weren't thrill-seeking. We were looking for an out, though I don't know what we needed to escape from—our mothers' fates, perhaps.

The next time I passed out was in college, a pursuit none of our moms had access to. By then, Cher's mother had started her own sewing business. I don't know if Dee Dee's mom had secret dreams. What I remember about my mom grabbing some independence was the smug look on Dad's face when she had to quit the sales job she could tolerate for only two weeks. Standing for hours was murder on the varicose veins childbearing had produced.

He wasn't smug when he sent me to college, a generous nod to the new world order unfolding before him, though he still loathed Gloria Steinem. Away at school, I was yo-yo dieting and fasting to deal with the freshman fifteen. I hated going back home with extra pounds my father would poke his finger at. "Putting on some weight?" He liked his women lean. Big boned, I would never be lean enough. One summer day at school, a salesman came to the trailer. I had a dog then, a good reason not to let the man in my yard. We spoke over the fence twined with morning glories. I stood in the sun wearing cutoffs, dark hair absorbing the heat. I think he was peddling religion. Then that familiar tingling beneath my skin, the woozy head, but no Cher or Dee Dee to gently lay me on the grass. No night sky that time either, just the man's voice calling from a distant place: "You okay? Hey. You all right?"

I don't like feeling vulnerable in public. Finally, I roused, the man's head a shadowy blur hovering over me. I gripped the fence and pulled myself up. "I'm fine." Black and white spots speckled the world. Alarm coated the man's face as I backed toward the porch. "My roommate's inside." A lie, but I wouldn't expose yet another vulnerability.

Myotonic goats don't really faint. When frightened, their legs merely go rigid and they topple over. It's a hereditary condition. They roll on their backs, legs stiff in the air, though I doubt they're reaching for stars. It's a quick recovery, mere seconds. A good thing. Still, I bet predators know exactly when to pounce before the goats rock their bodies back and forth, building momentum that will propel them to their still-stiff legs. I imagine them being dragged off by one of those inert legs into a wolf's den, the goats round-eyed at their impending demise.

My friend Marnie used to hate blood drives. The Red Cross would come to our Houston office and we'd line up in the break room for the cause. A good citizen, Marnie wanted to donate, and did, but she always passed out afterwards. She hated that. This was no squeamish woman. She was a hunter who could field dress, not Bambi, as she'd blurt when some asshole tried to put her in a girl box, but Bambi's daddy. It was her body that fainted, not her will.

I was never squeamish at the site of blood. It's snot that does me in. But I can clean and bandage lacerations. I removed stitches from that girl in Greece after her moped accident. I routinely gave blood in Houston, then for decades in West Virginia after I moved back home. I'd eat the cookies, drink the OJ. Until that day I sat in the recovery lounge. I was fifty then, sipping juice, when I felt suddenly woozy. I had enough sense to alert the volunteer walking by with the snack tray. "I think I'm going to pass out." Next thing I knew, I was on the floor, a phlebotomist kneeling over me. "You okay, hon?" She helped me sit up as the pinpricks in my extremities subsided. "Just stay put for a minute until you get your bearings."

I recovered and drove home, feeling sympathy for Marnie, but also feeling weak in body and fortitude.

The next day I called the Red Cross and told them I wouldn't be donating again. I blamed it on perimenopause, my hijacked body's new normal.

A few years later my ninety-year-old mother passed out on Christmas Eve. The family was gathered around my kitchen table, Mom beside me. My husband and I had made braciola, rolled meat stuffed with pine nuts and red peppers. In the middle of the meal, Mom's head tipped down. Her shoulder mashed into mine. I thought she was reaching for a dropped napkin, but that wasn't it. My sister took her home and the rest of us were supposed to go on as if nothing happened. My brother said, "It's okay. Chris has her." But all I could do as we ate pie and opened presents was quietly fret over Mom, her body frailer than her spirit. This woman who'd endured four miscarriages and five live births in nine years, and all with one ovary, she liked to brag. She was tough that way. Higher pain tolerance than my father ever had. The only silver lining to his early death was that he wouldn't have to endure old age. "Getting old ain't for sissies," Mom routinely said. That Christmas Eve likely wasn't her first fainting spell. If she had others, she didn't tell us. It wasn't just to keep us from worrying. It was to keep her in her home, alone. Finally, some independence.

She fainted a few more times. Once while eating oatmeal at her kitchen table; once while leaning over the counter making a meatball sandwich. Syncope, the doctors called it. A sudden drop in blood pressure. Not much to do about, really, after a battery of tests revealed things we already knew and some things we didn't. All we could do was continue fretting about her living alone, or being dragged off to a wolf's den by her arthritic leg.

The older and frailer she got, the clumsier I became. Anticipatory grief is fickle. Like that June day I sheered the end off my index finger with the new vegetable peeler. As my mother's daughter, I only seek medical attention if I see bone. But on that day, I couldn't stop the bleeding, so I bound the wound and drove to Urgent Care where they cauterized my fingertip. And I had just started playing the ukulele.

A year and a half later so much had changed. By then, a real wolfman had tricked his way into Mom's home. No longer safe, she moved into assisted living. Eighteen months after that a bad fall brought on her death. It's what she wanted, to be out of that traitorous body that caused her so much pain. And to be out of that facility that offered no privacy. My guilt about the move is still thick.

And then I did it again, sliced my finger while cutting bread for the squirrels. Same damn finger, too, and I'd just restarted playing the ukulele. Post-mortem grief is also fickle. I doused the cut with peroxide and drove to the walk-in clinic. No big deal, I kept saying to the intake person. Not even sure if it was stitch-worthy, if not for all the bleeding. The nurse prac came in, a lovely man named Kevin, who decided on liquid stitches that captivated me. "Can you buy them over-the-counter?" Seemed like something I should keep in my medicine cabinet.

I sat in a chair, arm draped over the table, while Kevin worked on the slice. Then I felt it come on: the woozy tingling. "I feel weird." My head tipped toward the floor as if I were going to scoop up a napkin.

When I came to, Kevin had one meaty arm strapped around my shoulder. I was still in my chair. "You with me?" Kevin offered a few gentle shakes. "You okay?" My head lolled as he jiggled me into consciousness. "Has this ever happened before?"

"Yes." My tongue felt thick. "Years ago when I gave blood."

"It's happened before," he said to dismiss the woman at the door with the wheelchair. To me he said, "Vasovagal syncope. Happens to a lot of people at the sight of blood."

I balked at the intimated weakness. "I'm not squeamish."

Kevin offered a cookie, a sip of water. Drew blood to check my sugar, which was fine.

"Sit here a minute until you feel better." He patted my hand and his was so, so warm. What I wanted was to go home and be alone, safe, like Mom would have done when she still had her own home.

Later, I Googled vasovagal syncope. It's not uncommon. It can be years between events, so I catalogued mine: college, perimenopause, sliced fingers. I don't count hyperventilating with Cher and Dee Dee in the woods. I still don't know exactly what we were escaping: womanhood, perhaps, or at least the version our mothers presented to us. Decades of accommodating others until we could finally have a minute to ourselves— for as long as we could keep it.

MARIE MANILLA

Marie Manilla is a graduate of the Iowa Writers' Workshop. Her novel *The Patron Saint of Ugly* won the Weatherford Award. *Shrapnel* received the Fred Bonnie Award for Best First Novel. Stories in her collection, *Still Life with Plums*, first appeared in the *Chicago Tribune, Prairie Schooner, Mississippi Review, Calyx*, and elsewhere. Her essays have appeared in *Word Riot, Cossack Review, Under the Sun, Hippocampus, Still*, and other journals.

Beginning to Breathe
excerpt from her forthcoming memoir *Sacred Catharsis*

KELLI HANSEL HAYWOOD

photo credit: Andrea Fekete

April 13th, strong wind producing storms moved through the mountains of eastern Kentucky. Here we live on flatter lands at the base of the hills, often along the beds of a creek. We call them hollers (hollows). I have found it often unfathomable to people outside of the region to know how difficult it is for us to obtain and maintain basic utilities. If you have never seen the terrain of central Appalachia, or lived in other very rural areas, it really is impossible to know. All of our electrical power lines run up and over the forest covered mountains, or through tree lined holler roads. We do not have options for utilities here as it is often one company that provides each service for things like internet and phone service. We have very little broadband infrastructure. Cell towers do not send signal capabilities into every holler either. After the storms, thousands in my area were without power. And because many still get their water from electrically pumped private wells, they were without water too.

For the next five days, we were without electricity, cell service, internet service, and landline service. In our rental home, we have a fireplace, but the warmth it provided was limited. Fortunately, my brother-in-law loaned us a gas powered generator and I did not lose my stocked refrigerator of food. It was incredibly cold though, and we had to keep the outside door in the kitchen cracked to run the gas generator from the back yard, which allowed more cold to seep in. It was still expected that my daughters complete their school work. So, assignments that could not be done on paper were incomplete. They were troopers though. Hardly complained.

It was hard to eat while cold. We spent days on the couch under blankets until the sun warmed up enough to be outside. We couldn't shower because there was no hot water. Heating water for a bath was impossible and I feared it was too cold anyway. I have Raynaud's Syndrome and that coupled with POTS made being cold very hard on my body. POTS is an autonomic nervous system dysregulation of unknown origin that affects the electrical workings of the heart. Among the symptoms are high and low blood pressure, dizziness, exhaustion, pain and shakiness, nausea, mental fog, and temperature deregulation on both the hot and cold spectrums. No matter what I did, I could not get warm.

About three days into the outage, my heart started showing signs of stress. My blood pressure was dipping dangerously low and I became lethargic. Worse symptoms than I had experienced in the past made themselves known. Along with the dangerously low blood pressure, my migraines became frequent, my entire body ached, I was constantly dizzy even when sitting, and I found myself having to spend days lying on the couch. Doctors, including my cardiologist, were not seeing patients outside of emergencies. I would have to wait another month to be seen unless I wanted to risk going through the ER at the largest local hospital.

When our power finally returned, the fatigue hung heavy on our bodies. I could feel the tightness it had created through my tissues. I imagined, then, what it must be like to be homeless. When you really have to push beyond feeling tired, until the tired is like a thick molasses coating your every movement. You have to stop caring about some things. Caring is too much. I bought a blood pressure monitor online, and decided that the thing I had to focus on was staying healthy. Nothing else could be done if I became sick from scattering too much of my energy scrambling toward undetermined outcomes.

Generally speaking, human beings don't like to be uncomfortable. Our biological systems are designed to achieve homeostasis, or a state of stability within the body when confronting ever changing external factors. Our brains, as the control center, are constantly seeking this stability and they develop patterns, based upon past experiences we have, that allow a quick return to that state regardless of what toll adherence to that pattern takes. It makes no difference if the stressor is losing your keys or running from a bobcat, the way the body responds physically is the same. Digestion slows. Heart rate increases. Unnecessary functions slow or stop completely. Blood is shunted to the major muscles needed to fight or flight.

Respiration becomes quick and shallow. Instinct kicks in over cognition. The more your body diverts to this state of being, the more patterned the response is in your body and the more readily you go there as a familiar reaction to everyday life. Thus, stress becomes chronic, and all the health related issues that go with that ensue. Various states of anxiety become the norm. The same is true for mental and emotional states of being. Prominent books like *The Body Keeps the Score: Brain, Mind, and Body in the Healing of Trauma* published in 2014 by Bessel van der Kolk, which examine all the latest research in neurobiology, studies of trauma response, and the science of neuroplasticity explain this well. Every major event in our lives that produces an emotional response, or an accumulation of repeating minor adverse events, creates physical distress and holding patterns. These patterns and holdings are the cause of many illnesses and chronic pain over time. In the most basic terms, when we are happy we laugh. When we are sad, we cry. When we are angry, we yell. It is easy to see that emotion and physical response are tied. It is hard to discern what comes first, the emotion or the physical expression.

The science behind the mind and body connection is fascinating. However, the philosophical study of yoga and yoga practice have identified this for centuries on end. Patanjali, the credited author of the ancient text the Yoga Sutras discussed this principle long before there was science to prove it. The sutras, concise statements of thought much like a proverb in the Bible, dealing with karma (Sanskrit word meaning any action or activity that produces a result) and samskara (Sanskrit word meaning the patterns or imprints of our experiential conditioning) clearly coincide with the science on the topic. Anything that we experience or otherwise consume whether it be living in a home devoid of love, or watching a particularly violent movie, leaves an energetic impression within our body-mind. These impressions cause biases that are accessed unconsciously. These biases inform our developing opinions and ways of being based upon the most common experiences and the major traumas of our lives.

An example of this would be my great grandmother's phobia of birds. I never understood why she loathed even the mention of birds, until she told me the story of preparing a chicken for the table. Her job was plucking the feathers. She dunked the chicken in a boiling pot of water to loosen the feathers from the follicles. Suddenly, some of the feathers caught fire and the fat from the skin of the chicken combined with the fire to ignite the rest of the feathers melting some of them into the skin of my grandmother's hands and arms. She said she'd never forget the pain and the smell of the feathers. She found herself unable to like any bird again.

This truth is easy to understand even without being a scientist, psychologist, or therapist. It plays out in our lived experience with every breath we take. The churning of our stomach while watching a horror movie. The sudden intake of breath as we slam on the brakes when the car ahead of us abruptly stops without warning. The irritation we feel at our neighbor's barking dog. And, yes, even the good things, like the flush of our face when someone tells us the light of the sun makes our eyes look especially beautiful. The easiest way to think of it is that our brains and our bodies are intimate lovers, playing out their relationship every moment just outside of our awareness of them.

It becomes clear then, that if we want to be well and change the discomfort we feel in the day to day experience of life we have to be ready and willing to displace the familiar and get outside of our comfort zones. It is in our body and mind's innate ability to adapt to new scenarios that change is made. Therefore, we sometimes have to create the scenario by changing the habits and responses that no longer serve us as we become conscious of them When we are feeling dis-ease, the abnormal has become normal. Discomfort and the surface management of it has become comfortable. It is the expectation of our days instead of the exception. It has become a routine. The pattern. For change to be possible, we have to take the necessary steps to dig past the topsoil of our daily routines, and into the rich earth that really makes things grow. There will be rocks, old scraps of lives lived on that land before we came, roots galore, and perhaps trickles of water penetrating through it all to find flow. Getting to this place where we are willing to purposefully make ourselves uncomfortable for growth doesn't come easily. Most of us need an upset or an impetus that is rather strong. Had COVID-19 not completely upended our world, would I have noticed how comfortable I had become my routine?

This routine was requiring a layer of engagement that allowed me to avoid the issues that kept creeping into my reality at inopportune moments. It was enough of a distraction to make these repeating themes of struggle in my life look as if they were my luck, but I knew better. I just had to figure it out. Coming too that awareness took life as I knew it to not be possible.

It took my getting sick, worrying for the wellbeing of my children, being very emotionally unsettled, and fearful of my ability to sustain the effort that was required to find our way out of this mess without losing our stability, for me to come back to the tools I had gained through my study of yoga and my undertaking it as a spiritual practice. Things like mindfulness, breath, and moving with real awareness were no longer something touched on in a class, or considered in my practice until I became too distracted by chasing the next, more exciting goal on my agenda. They were something I had to use in order not to lose myself and find equanimity so that I could do what needed to be done. Then, they helped me see that it was time to take the next step in my personal journey of self healing and growth. I was being asked by my own body-mind to take them on as the practice. For, if I didn't, only a vapor of my true self was presenting in this life, and to exist in that way was a disservice to myself, my daughters, and the world. It would mean that the fear I had embodied as a child would win, and the gifts I carry in my unique form would be hidden from those who could use them. It would mean that if fear won, my life experience would be that which I dreaded - being abandoned, rejected, lonely, a constant struggler, and offering nothing of worth.

The next turn of events in 2020, brought forward a new responsibility for me to pull it together and not only survive, but to allow myself to thrive. The 8 minutes and 46 seconds of video that documented the killing death of Mr. George Floyd, a 46 year old black man suspected of using a counterfeit bill, at the hands of Minneapolis, Minnesota city police and the protests against racism and civil unrest that followed and continues as I write, demands that every breath we take be for the sake of love and the will that is found in our hearts. "I can't breathe," Mr. Floyd begged. He begged for his life's given right to breathe. Breath, or prana in the language of yoga, is the life force. Life begins and ends with breath. If we continue to draw breath, but cannot find in us the will to breathe life with a gratitude that drives us to fully embrace it, of what use is it that we breathe at all? We need to remember Mr. Floyd and the countless others who have found themselves begging for breath.

The theme of 2020 seems to be breath. The shortage of ventilators to tend to those experiencing the most severe cases of COVID-19 infection. The shortage of PPE (personal protective equipment) for the healthcare workers who willingly draw breath in the same room as those struggling with this virus. The last words of Mr. Floyd as he was strangled to death by a white man's knee who's malice and fear was emboldened by a uniform. Even those protesting the wearing of masks by the general public in active public gatherings, or by simply choosing not to wear one, exercising their born right to breathe unimpeded as they see fit through their individual conscience. I could not ignore the call to explore what it means to be alive through the practice of yoga and its own call for us to use and experience our breath to let go of the illusions that our trauma, conditioning, and fears hold us in, keeping us small and ineffective. I cannot undo our collective path simply because my heart wants better for all of us. What I can do though is write a new story for myself. As long as I continue to draw breath, I can see that it counts toward the best of my potential as a human. In living and sharing the sweetness of that potential, perhaps the suffering of the collective can be eased.

In the following chapters, I'm going to share the ways in which I have devoted myself to the work of true wellbeing. How I have used movement and mindfulness practices to begin to unlock the places in my body where the tragedies of my life were stored so that I may release them, giving them back to the energies that transmute our existence in ways best for us. I am not giving an elaborate new system, nor have

I created an entirely different set of practices to learn and attempt to integrate into life. We have access to enough information and eons of recommendations for effective physical, mental, and spiritual practices. It could easily happen that we spend our entire lives trying to find the answers in all the sources provided to us, so much so that we never begin to apply what we are learning to know that we have found what we are looking for. It becomes obvious that what we seek is not in new methods, adopting someone else's lifestyle, or finding a guru or master teacher. The answers we seek are to be found within ourselves. Our minds, our spirits, our bodies.

I have not discovered or improved anything. I am simply sharing my personal story. This is the narrative of an average person in daily life applying already existing practices to heal in the midst of a global crisis. This is the rarely seen part. We often get descriptions of systems or we see the results of a person's practice, but we seldom are privy to how it looks applied to a real life day in and day out.

I am a mother, a yogi, and a writer. I am not unlike you. In this story, you will read my perspective and interpretation of many spiritual and philosophical principles pertaining to the practices of yoga (asana), breath (pranayama), and mindfulness. Most importantly, I will share how the scaffolding of the chakra system and principles of yoga practice allows me to unfurl the narrative of my life that led me to an identity that held me back from living my purpose and understanding that I have something to contribute. Through sharing this with you, I will also include some of this life story and the old conclusions that held me down. It is my hope that in so doing, you will find that you are not alone, and that if a holler kid from the hills of southeastern Kentucky can take on this mission to live in the truth of self, that you can too, if your heart wills it so. All we have to do is start by noticing the stillness in the pause between breaths, and on the very next inhalation choose to breathe in your freedom. Ready? Breathe.

Kelli Hansel Haywood is an author, public speaker/teacher, and mother of three daughters in the mountains of southeastern, Kentucky. Kelli's most recent published works can be found in *Appalachian Reckoning: A Region Responds to Hillbilly Elegy* from West Virginia University Press (2019), in various editions of *Pine Mountain Sand & Gravel*, as well as among other online journals and magazines, including long form journalism, radio journalism, creative nonfiction, fiction, and blogs. The piece featured in this journal is an excerpt from her forthcoming book titled *Sacred Pause*.

RUNNING IN THE HALLS
TALES OF A WANNABE GIRL BY LARA LILLIBRIDGE

The boys carried pens in the back pockets of their jeans in fifth grade, and I did, too. Sometimes they broke when I sat on them and left a blue stain on my pocket the size of a quarter, but if I kept them in my pocket I could run faster in the halls between classes without dropping anything. I liked to run. I liked the breeze flowing off of the backs of kids racing alongside me and the slide of my sneakers on the old asbestos tile floor. I knew I could get a detention if caught, and I liked that too—the adrenaline rush when I saw a teacher and the practiced skill of skidding to a walk the minute I spotted one.

We carried our pens in our pockets and we ran in the halls and we battled it out on the playground, the boys and I. There was kickball, and chasing and hitting the boys who needed to be chased and hit. And there was see-saw with the girls, and a steel balance beam only one foot off the ground that I was very bad at, no matter how much I practiced.

Girls sat in their chairs nicely at school and only raised their hands slightly, resting their elbows on their desks. They didn't wave their arms or go, "oh, oh, oh!" when they knew the answer like the boys and I did. Waving my arms and making monkey noises added a modicum of excitement to the classroom, and it burned off a little bit of that energy that was always inside, begging for release. I didn't like to brush my hair, but I liked it to wear it long so that I looked like a girl. I loved the purple skirts my dad bought me for my tenth birthday, and I loved roller skating to Michael Jackson music. I loved wearing barrettes and I had one with long ribbons that flew behind me as I skated. I didn't want to be a boy, not even a little bit, but it was obvious to me that boys had a lot more fun, and I was in favor of fun. I took fun wherever I could find it.

When I sat in class, I itched to get up and move; my body hummed with the need for release from the confines of my blue plastic chair. School was boring and made my brain hurt, or it was frustrating and made my cheeks hot with the effort not to cry because I felt so dumb. Above all else, I did not want to be dumb. I was a child of extremes and running and kickball and roller skating were the places where I wasn't bored or dumb or lonely. They made everything tolerable inside me, even if I was sweaty and out of breath and my jeans had ink stains from carrying my pens in my pockets.

But I knew this wasn't what I was supposed to be. I knew I was supposed to raise my hand only halfway and not go, "oh, oh, oh!" and never run in the halls. I knew that the girls at school didn't really like me and I no longer had a best friend, after having the same one since first grade. Dawn and I had gotten into a fight and she replaced me with a girl named Carrie who carried her pens in her purse and never ran in the halls.

It wasn't until sixth grade that I stopped jumping up and down when I knew the answer in class. On the last day of school, I wore my mint green tank top with the pink flower on the chest. It was my favorite shirt, but as I waved my hand in the air I saw that I was growing fine hairs in my armpit. For the rest of the day I kept my arm clamped tightly to my body and only raised my hand halfway, resting my elbow on my desk like the rest of the girls. I ran home and shaved but I never trusted my armpits not to betray me again. Puberty broke my spirit in a way that all my teachers could not.

The summer after sixth grade my best "boy" friend asked if he could kiss me and if, "Lefty [his left hand] could have a field day." I ran from his house laughing, knowing I was curious but not ready for that. I liked the attention and the power of the idea of dating, but I didn't know how to say that I just wanted to sing songs on the bus and hold hands and hit him with my purse when he irritated me, because that was all I could handle. These new feelings were too intense and I didn't know what to do with them and they made me anxious, so instead of answering yes or no I ran the mile back to my mother's house.

Seventh grade started and I never ran in the halls. The new school clothes I had been so proud of were all wrong, my "slacks" frumpish compared to the other girls' designer jeans. I carried a comb and checked my hair in the mirror at school, hating how I looked with my big glasses and braces and the accidentally too-short bangs that I had cut myself a decade after most kids learned not to cut their own hair. I had a curling iron and tried to catch up with the other girls but I felt like my feminine skills were a lifetime behind theirs. I stopped hitting boys with my purse or with anything else.

I blamed my mother for not making me come down from the maple tree in the backyard. She should have forced me to be feminine. If she had been a different kind of mother—one who shaved her legs, read fashion magazines, and knew how to work a curling iron—I could have passed as a girl. She would have fixed my hair and glossed my lips and known just what clothes to buy for me. But now I know differently. My mother just stood back and let me be who I was—a tomboy girl who cared more about riding bikes and climbing trees than about pretty clothes. And what was normal anyway? I played with Barbies, my bedroom was pink, and I wore dresses when I wanted to. The trappings of girlhood were not enough to change my soul.

My mother said I had to play a team sport, so I signed up for track because it was the only team you didn't have to try out for. We ran every day. I finally saw what my legs could do, and I liked how strong they were and how the wind cooled my forehead and it was as good as running in the halls ever was, better even, because I ran like that every day and sometimes I even won.

High school started. I wore spike heels and miniskirts, and I smoked in the bus loop before school. My grades fell and suddenly, I was not eligible to run track anymore. I was dejected, but I told no one. Until then, I had counted on track to save me, to rewind me back to the girl I used to be. When I was finally able to compete again, several years later, I went to only two practices before I quit. I was a regular smoker by then and I couldn't't honestly sign the tobacco-free pledge the coach handed out. I didn't know anyone, I was too self-conscious, and I didn't like people looking at me anyway.

At my last track practice, we did a one-legged hopping exercise. We stood in lines, like a relay race. As I hopped, I passed the kids who had started before me. I was so fast that the coach made everyone else stop and watch me, all one hundred and twenty kids staring as I hopped across the gymnasium floor. I was proud and ashamed all at once. I never went back after that, but I wish I had. I liked being the girl who was the best at hopping even though there was no one-legged hopping event in high school track and field. But maybe I was only so good at hopping because I could swing my hips, and maybe my hip swinging would betray to the other kids that I was no longer a virgin. These were the athletes who had top grades and didn't smoke in the bus loop outside school. I didn't want them to know that I was dirty.

I didn't want to care if the good girls liked me anyway. I didn't like them, and I didn't want to be like them. I could tell that their lives had been too gentle: too safe and too rewarding. I knew this because of their neatly pressed clothing and naturally flawless skin, and from their shiny, bouncy hair. I knew they must be boring because they smiled too often. I was afraid they would never like me if they saw who I was underneath my leather jacket. If they ever got to know me, they would see that I was just a wannabe girl. There's a certain kind of girl who can wear sweatpants and T-shirts and look like a newly planted flower ready to blossom. Real girls have a way of delicately tucking a lock of hair behind one ear, a way of dropping their chin when they smile and never telling off-color jokes. There is something about this type of female that makes a person want to open the door for them or hold out their chair at the table. They must have learned this grace while I was running in the halls.

I never looked fragile or in need of protection. My gaze was always too direct, my energy too strong, my gait too awkward. I was the kind of girl who could do anything a boy could do, but I secretly dreamed of being rescued by Prince Charming. I was the kind of girl for whom no one held the door open. If they had, I would only have walked awkwardly through it with my cheeks burning because I knew I was an impostor. I was not someone worth holding the door for, and not someone who needed the door held open for her. I did not know how to erase all of the boyishness from my soul and emerge feminine.

I studied the girls at school and the women in magazines like a teenaged Jane Goodall, trying to learn their culture. I found that the girls I simultaneously scorned and envied would often smile back if I smiled first. I learned that they did not hate me or fear me, or really spend much time thinking about me one way or the other. I might have been an odd girl, but the rest of them had their own lives and friends and other things to think about. I learned to sit demurely and gossip viciously, and to put on makeup with a steady hand. None of this was remarkably interesting, but I did not know how else to be a girl. So, I tried to remember to cross my legs when I sat, and practiced walking like a model, and was so bored that I thought my brain might turn to jelly, leak out of my ear and run down my neck.

After a while, I became indistinguishable from the other girls at school. I finally achieved my lifelong dream—to be just like everyone else. Learning to look feminine wasn't all that hard. Learning to feel feminine was a different matter entirely. It was out of my grasp. My energy was wrong.

I knew how to sit quietly and flash a fetching smile, but I was not always willing to constrain myself to such behavior for very long. Somehow I projected "one of the boys" no matter what I wore, but let's face it, that's more fun, anyway.

If I knew that I did not conform to one of the opposites of boy and girl but instead was a mix in-between, why did I fight it so? I could not see myself as beautiful unless I was feminine, and I did not want to see myself as anything but beautiful. There is power in a high-heeled boot and short skirt that will never be matched by jeans and sneakers. Ugly girls have no power at all.

I did not realize that a significant part of my beauty is contained in my androgyny—in my sharp cheekbones and strong shoulders. I needed someone else to see me for who I was without my artifice and still find me beautiful. Only then would I give myself permission to explore who I could be if no one else cared, and finally allow the thought that perhaps that wannabe-girl part of me was quite possibly my best self, instead of the passable feminine version I had perfected.

BIO

Lara Lillibridge is the author of two memoirs, *Mama, Mama, Only Mama: An Irreverent Guide for the Newly Single Parent—from Divorce and Dating to Cooking and Crafting, All While Raising the Kids and Maintaining Your Own Sanity (Sort Of)* & *Girlish: Growing Up in a Lesbian Home* a Foreword INDIES Book of the Year Awards Finalist. Lara co-edited an anthology with Andrea Fekete entitled *Feminine Rising: Voices of Power and Invisibility* (2019), which took the Silver Award for Foreword Review's Indie Book of the Year in women's studies. Lara Lillibridge is a graduate of West Virginia Wesleyan College's MFA program in Creative Nonfiction. In 2016 she won *Slippery Elm Literary Journal's* Prose Contest & The American Literary Review's Contest in Nonfiction. She also was a finalist in both *Black Warrior Review's* Nonfiction Contest and DisQuiet's Literary Prize in Creative Nonfiction. She is a member of the reading panel for *Hippocampus Magazine* & was awarded their Literary Citizen of the Year for 2019. Lara judged AWP's Intro Journals Project for 2019 & was recently selected as a mentor for their Writer to Writer program.

LOOK

CLOSER

POETRY

ACE BOGGESS | PAULETTA HANSEL | JODI MCMILLIAN
MARY B. MOORE

photo credit: Taryn Conn, "Cascade Transparency"

JODI MCMILLIAN

AMERICAN STORMS

The curtains are closed.
Home.
Behind the tattered fabric
that I feel safe inside but still less so than before.
Here behind that window that door, those old timbers,
vigilantly holding the world out, day after day.
Home.
The wind blows and the shell holds its defense.
The lightning and winds threaten to break it all apart.
But the windows don't shatter after rattling a war cry to the night.
Rain abuses the metal roof.
But no dampness is allowed inside.
I hold onto myself, my skin, my shell,
my eyes, the windows, my bones, the timbers,
my cells, the curtains.
Thank you for holding on, keeping me intact
even as my windows rattle,
and my roof is banged upon by these American storms.

BREATHING

If the light was young,

if this was not all shared air

we have shared for millions of years.

If the water was not the same water the earth has circulated since the beginning,

then maybe, maybe I could believe in individualism

or authoritarianism.

But the act of breathing

is a socialist, collaborative and

collective experience.

MARY B. MOORE

DISCOURSE ON MASKING

Sure, the intersection mandates
hesitation, at least vigilance, a form

civility takes, an allowing the other
to pass without fatality. Most tolerate it,

even assume it, a ground.
These and similar wordless agreements

allow the softer civil beauties: not
axing the neighbor's dogwood,

its pink flowers held flat out
like hors d'oeuvres on plates, or their maples

uncrinkling their almost sheer leaves;
not trampling those impatiens

the all-of-a-size river stones ring,
delineating the bed someone weeds, tends.

Stopping, you could choose to think you surrendered
your free-wheeling to a sign,

but isn't it just a sundering,
a dividing, like allowing each impatien

and maple tree, even the round stones, their own
small pasture in air? The Malibu bears

its mortal cargo, its engine's power
still numbered by horse,

as the red Infinity nears and brakes:
Nobody need forsake

their right to be. It's a constant
music, this toleration, like the bass line,

the undertow, that grounds and enables harmony.
You might find a kind of sense,

even ease, in being affable, leaving
room for trespass, forgive and alive.

Loss of will? Hardly. We're like little gods,
or the many horses love rides.

PAULETTA HANSEL

March 22, 2020

Friend, did you see the sun,
        a gift, remembered brightness
at the end of the day.
        I stood at the fence talking
to a tree, my husband reported
        from his window;
from my view, to a neighbor
        about raised garden beds and squirrels
who keep no distance
        from our tulips and tomatoes.
How sweet to complain
        of ordinary losses,
the stubbornness of squirrels,
        a lilac tree that has again this year
refused us blossoms.

April 2, 2020

Dear friend,
        On March 26, you wrote,
With every curse a little blessing.
        I've said myself there is no shadow
without light. But does it work the other way?
        On yesterday's walk—from the neighbor's tall grasses,
a sudden flash of mottled brown. Midstride,
        I grab my husband's arm as a hawk flies
past our faces to another neighbor's pine.
        A blessing, surely.
This time together in the greening spring,
        rounding the corner on our urban sidewalk
to see what we otherwise would not.
        Not so much a blessing for the mouse.

April 8, 2020

Dear friend, the days pass quickly now.
        Did you think you'd see these words
from me, who just last week—or was it two—
        wrote nostalgia of restaurants and stores?
My husband and I venture
        farther now from home,
shy creatures of the underbrush,
        with face masks and wipes.
I admit to you my inclination
        is to outrun the black dog,
though at 60 I outwalk it.
        Fifty miles last week, my wristwatch says.
I could have walked to Fowlers Fork
        and back again, by now.
I could have stood six feet downstream,
        skipped a stone to you.
The best stone skipper
        chooses her rock with the jeweler's attention.
As in anything, it's practice
        that makes an art of love.

ACE BOGGESS

REALITY

Want my life a tensely-plotted film—
noirish but in 90s-slacker style.
Thrills of bodies, a missing prize,
a golden gun—give me those
from safety of my room.
I'm a man of big dreams,
small actions, as though I've found
a cure for the virus &
don't know who to call.
Besides, who would believe me
sitting here wearing
dark sweatpants & red,
white, & blue Hawaiian shirt?
Part of me apprehends I am the
answer
to important questions no one asks,
or a speck of interstellar dust
lacking any atmosphere
through which to fall & burn.

"WHERE HAVE I MISPLACED MY HEART?"

—Li-Young Lee, "Dreaming of Hair"

I'm always losing it, forgetting, leaving it
folded in a breast pocket of the red & gold flannel
I wore last Tuesday. It's been through the wash,
though I've never taken it to the cleaners.
It sometimes ends up in a drawer I haven't opened in years
next to photographs of friends, lovers, conspirators—
also lost—or buried under bottles of expired vitamins.
How did it get left in the car that died on the highway?
The hole in an oak out front as if squirreled away
by those nesting there? I can't say I miss it
when it's gone, until I do, then ransack my history
for clues. Who did I overlook that might have kept it
when I left? Why did I let it fall to the floor
as if it wouldn't shatter like a snow globe?
Does it matter that I stash it in a cold lockbox?
As I turn the key, I know I will find it
has escaped those suffocating walls.

ANDRÉA FEKETE

TREES CATCH WHITE

branches swish, bend, tangle.
Train outside the trailer window
stuck on a high note,
sings of coal miners,
bodies deep—black caves.

Next door, a baby's cry.
A dog's bark.
A shotgun blast echoes
among the hills.

Ice feathers across the window,
the night—a blue shade.
Fog glimmers, seems to crack
a white slit in the orange throat
along the horizon.

First Appeared in *Borderlands: Texas Poetry Review* Volume 40

ABOUT THE POETS

Ace Boggess is author of the novel *A Song Without a Melody* (Hyperborea Publishing, 2016) and several books of poetry including *The Prisoners* (Brick Road Poetry Press, 2014), *Ultra Deep Field* (Brick Road). His writing has appeared in *Harvard Review, Mid-American Review, RATTLE, River Styx, Chiron Reviwe, North Dakota Quarterly* and many other journals. He lives in Charleston, West Virginia.

Andréa Fekete's literary novel of the historical coal mine wars, *Waters Run Wild*, (2018) explores women's & immigrant life in the coal camps of West Virginia. Her poetry & fiction appear in many journals & anthologies such as *Chiron Review, Borderlands: Texas Poetry Review, The Kentucky Review, The Montucky Review, The Smithville Journal, The Adirondack Review, ABZ*, and in anthologies such as *Eyes Glowing at the Edge of the Woods: Fiction & Poetry from West Virginia*, among others. She co-curated F*eminine Rising: Voices of Power & Invisibility* (2019) a collection of poetry & essays from women writers from around the globe. The book took the Silver in Foreword Review's Indie Book of the Year in Women's Studies. An excerpt from her unpublished novel *Native Trees* was a finalist in *Still: The Journal*'s 2019 Fiction contest. She taught college English & writing for almost 15 years at multiple universities in West Virginia, Kentucky & Ohio. She currently seeks literary representation.

Pauletta Hansel's featured poems are from the chapbook *Friend* (Dos Madres Press, 2020), epistolary poems written in the early days of the Covid-19 pandemic. Pauletta is author of eight poetry collections including *Coal Town Photograph* and *Palindrome*, winner of the 2017 Weatherford Award for best Appalachian Poetry. Her writing has been widely anthologized and featured in print and online journals including O*xford American, Rattle, The Writer's Almanac, American Life in Poetry, Verse Daily. Appalachian Journal, Appalachian Review, Cincinnati Review,* and *Still: The Journal*, among others. Pauletta is past Managing Editor of *Pine Mountain Sand & Gravel* and was Cincinnati's first Poet Laureate, 2026-2018.

Jodi Mcmillian lives in the small Appalachian city of Charleston West Virginia. For twenty years, she worked as a private licensed massage therapist. Since March of 2020, she has abstained from work for the safety of her community. She's been instead training as a virtual Health and Wellness Coach. She assists her community in health-related matters through phone calls rather than in-person sessions. She continues to journal and write poetry, enjoy walks along the Kanawha River, hiking in the mountains, African and World dancing, being with friends and family outside, gardening and eating delicious food with her husband.

Professor Emeritus, Mary B. Moore, retired from Marshall University iun 2014. Her second full-length collection, *Flicker,* won the 2016 Dogfish Head Poetry award (judges, Carol Frost, Baron Wormser, and Jan Beatty), and her chapbook *Eating the Light,* won Sable Books' 2016 award (judge, Allison Joseph): both appeared that year. Cleveland State published *The Book of Snow* (1998). *Georgia Review, Poem/Memoir/Story, Cider Press Review, Drunken Boat,* and *Birmingham Poetry Review* have published recent poems. She won Nimrod's 2017 Pablo Neruda Poetry Contest's Second Place Award, and poems are forthcoming in that journal, and in *The Nasty Woman Anthology,* Cider Press Review, and Minerva Rising, among others.

BECOMING

INTERVIEWS WITH ENGAGING HUMANS

RON HOUCHIN, POET
Retired Major richard Ojeda, II
Chet Lowther, artist

photo credit: Taryn Conn

Interview with Ron Houchin, poet and author

Andréa Fekete: Do you consider yourself an Appalachian writer? Why or why not?

Ron Houchin: At one time in my early years, I hated the term Appalachian Writer. It felt too limiting when I was an undergrad at Marshall in the '60s. It smacked of regional to me then and that meant, felt like it meant, limited and not fit for the larger world outside the "prisoning hills." Now, I revel in it, now I understand that all writing is regional. All writers, whether they aware of it or not, are impacted and influenced by where they grew up, lived, and the language of that region—not to mention the religion..

AF: I know you visit Ireland quite frequently. You also have a long-term relationship with an Irish publisher, Salmon Press, who've published many of your poetry collections. 5, I think? Could you tell us more about developing long-term relationships with a publisher and why Ireland? Ireland seems to be a land very special to you.

RH: I plan to go again in the spring or early summer. I've been there in every season. With an average temperature of 59 degrees Fahrenheit, it is rarely freezing or blistering. The people there, the land, the history, and prehistory are all just what I love about the human race and this land we survive on: beautiful in spirit both the people and the land. They have their problems and deal with them in their way, which seems to me very human and humane the more I get to know them—that's something we in the US could benefit from more of. Even though they have an amazing amount of legends and superstitions informing their sense of self and their place in the world, they see much more clearly and honestly than most cultures I've known. So, this next visit, whenever it occurs, will be my 30th. If I hadn't gone there so many times, I could have a nice house, yacht, and maybe a trophy wife. Kidding, of course. The good news is I am interested in none of that. I want experiences and understanding that I seem only to get in the writing and traveling—seeing things from other perspectives, other than my own.

An underdog country that has been bullied and tortured for over 600 years, Ireland amazes me at how much they have influenced the world, especially the world of literature and the arts. Why wouldn't I want to gain and keep a relationship with an Irish publisher? Jessie Lendennie, the director of Salmon Publishing, is known for her egalitarian approach to publishing both women and men from Ireland and all over the world. A long relationship with a publisher is a kind of love affair, if you're lucky, and I am plenty lucky. It's an affair of minds. The writer loves the work the publisher does and the publisher loves the writing. I've had other books done by other publishers: Louisiana State University Press, Wind Publications for the other of my 8 books. And Main Street Rag for the novella. But above all of this, when you are reading in a foreign country, at their request, and one of their publishing houses comes to you after the reading and says something like, "I really liked what you read. You should send me a book manuscript," and you do, and it gets published THERE (in Ireland already famous for poetry and poets such as Yeats and Heaney, and Beckett and Synge, and Behan and many more), when you could not get a book done in your own country, how can you not feel lucky, stay with them, and do what you can to see them thrive?

AF: Does Ireland or Appalachia provide you with a sense of place in your work? Do you believe a sense of place is necessary for a poet? How does it manifest in your own work?

RH: I know this is not the popular, preferred view these days, and it may seem somehow inconsistent after all that about Ireland; but I feel all this sense of place is a bit overblown. I mean, I was born in National City, California, a small town that has since been absorbed by San Diego. Had I stayed there, I'd be influenced by the great Southwest more than anyplace else. Sense of place should never be, at least for me, a kind of cheerleading, a Go Appalachia! attitude of my writing. I hope it never is in the poetry and the fiction. In the nonfiction, that's another matter. Sense of place does not mean a sense of loyalty or nationalism or regionalism, but just a matter of whether when writing, the warehouse of images you've accumulated through a lifetime of observation is filled with mountain laurel or bougainvillea that pops up when you need a floral reference or image. If your senses are working, and you pay attention to them, you will have to have a sense of place in your writing—it's inevitable. It's not an accomplishment.

AF: When I visited Ireland, I felt there are similarities to my homeland of West Virginia. West Virginia is home of the coal mine wars with a long history of workers' uprisings. I noted those shared quality of love of land and a deep reverence for their history of resistance. Do you see these kinds of parallels and if not these- then what? Do these aspects of Irish culture inform your poetry?

RH: Someone once said, if you want to be brilliant, you have to pay attention to the Universe. Who wants to read the poetry of a dullard? I shouldn't say that. It may have already become a hipster fad. Nonetheless, I try to pay attention to whatever comes to my window, so to speak, so I can't help but feel that West Virginia is the Ireland of the US, and Washington—the government—is England. Look at the example of Ireland, they have had the English boot in their face for over half the millennium. They are getting along very nicely out from under that boot. WV resorted to violence when necessary, just as did Ireland—and as violence is often wont to do, it got out of hand. How can this not inform what I write? I come from an area that has a history of being raped and plundered and I go out as a young writer and find and fall in love with a country that has even greater history with the same sort of treatment.

AF: Does your poetry reflect where you are when you write? I've heard some writers say they only wrote about home when they are away.

RH: I never know what I am going to write until about a nanosecond before I start writing it. As much as possible, I write wherever I go. I am a strong believer in anamorphisms, the way changing our position so often changes what and how we see. Looking at something straight-on will change dramatically when we see it from the side. For this analogy, Home is viewing and thinking straight-on, and anywhere else, even your neighbor's back yard, is viewing from the side. If that makes sense.

AF: What's your process from idea to finished poem?

RH: An Irish writer whom I love both in her work and her person is Paula Meehan. In a workshop in the '90s she once said how we must "invigilate" our work. Didn't know that was a word, but it makes sense. You know what a vigil is. You have to keep vigil over your writing. When I am working on something, which is most of the time—thank the gods and goddesses—I am rather absent minded about the rest of the world. I am obsessed with whatever idea has me in its grip

I may start out way over here in the dull twilight of some thought, but if I keep with it, I will finish in the brightness of noon—if I am lucky, also. Mastery is staying with it as it stays with you. It's a kind of loyalty that never ends. I regularly change poems that are 10, 20 years old. Often I change a poem that's already been published in journal or book form. I forget whom am I paraphrasing now, Da Vinci or someone, who said, "A painting is never finished only abandoned." Something like that. I could go back right now and change any number of poems from yesterday or a decade ago. And I probably will.
What advice do you have for poets of all ages? Young or emerging poets?

Same as what Rilke gave once to a young poet: If you don't have to do it, don't. It won't get you in to heaven or keep you from hell. It may make life worth the living, but only if you are crazy in love with it.

Perseverance is paramount for emerging or emerged—unfortunately that makes the whole process sound like a bowel movement. I started writing before I'd conquered the language. I couldn't construct a clear, grammatical sentence, let alone a paragraph. I had a huge learning curve. I'd been a semi-criminal through much of my public-school days and hadn't paid much attention, so when I entered Marshall University in 1966, I had to hit the ground running to avoid being drafted. That was my wake up call, being a high school graduate and realizing that my country wanted me to go half way or more around the world and kill strangers who couldn't have harmed us here with all their efforts combined. I guess what I am saying is that it takes great motivation to keep at it.
But look at the Universe. Just one big explosion and it is still going strong.

Ron Houchin, a retired public-school teacher in the Appalachian region of southernmost Ohio, taught for thirty years. Though raised on the remote banks of the Ohio River in Huntington, West Virginia, he has travelled throughout Europe, Canada, and the U.S. His work has appeared in *Poetry Ireland Review, The Stinging Fly, The Southwest Review, Appalachian Heritage, The New Orleans Review,* and over two hundred other venues. He has been awarded an Ohio Arts Council Grant for teachers of the arts, a tutorial fellowship to teach in a Dublin writing workshop, a poetry prize from Indiana University, as lll as a book of the year award from the Appalachian Writers' Association. His poems have been featured on Verse Daily. He has published three collections with Salmon Poetry.

Interview with Retired Major Richard Ojeda, II.

Andréa Fekete: You've been through more than most can imagine. Not only were you brutally beaten just days before your senatorial election to stop that run for office, but you survived multiple deployments overseas where you led troops through unimaginable horrors. You cleaned up Haiti which I understand was one of the most grotesque sights in the history of tsunamis. What is your mindset when you're in a situation of chaos that requires calm and clarity? How do you get there?

Major Richard Ojeda: Great training is the key. Realistic training. Tough training that makes you think, to find ways around problems. Nothing can prepare you for death! You train to deal with chaos, but nothing can truly prepare you for the real thing. We train for casualties. Before I deployed to Iraq on my first combat tour, I coordinated a group of my troops that I knew would be with me on missions outside of the wire on daily operation where they were sent to a civilian Emergency Medical Technicon (EMT) course. My thoughts were that if one of us got shot I wanted to ensure we'd have troops that can handle serious cases. One of my NCO's administered a tracheotomy on the side of the road after a Vehicular Borne Improvised Explosive Device (VBIED) that killed 1 and injured 4.

As far as remaining in control during chaotic experiences, it comes with maturity. The training places you in scenarios that create muscle memory that allows you to complete tasks under extreme duress. This does not mean that everyone can be successful under fire. People get relieved because they prove they do not have the capability to lead when times get tough. I'm just lucky I guess to have the ability to turn off distractors when in dangerous situations.

Fekete: You stated that in Afghanistan, it was just you and two other Americans conducting missions by yourselves without back-up. Can you describe your strategy for survival? What keeps you hopeful? How do you maintain high levels of emotional and mental strength in such situations?

Ojeda: The key is to try and always keep your wits about any situation. On your down time you need to stay sharp. Conduct physical training on your own which keeps you strong and confident. In Afghanistan, I tried not to focus on the dangerous situation we were in and just focus on the mission itself. We were trained to do our job and we were equipped to defend ourselves, but we knew the most important thing that we had was secrecy as to not allow anyone to know our schedule and to know when we were going to show up. This kept the enemy off of their toes. Trust is another key issue. I had to know that my two NCO's that were with me were competent and ready for whatever came our way. I had 11 other soldiers that I could have taken with me, but they were not trained to conduct key leader engagements with Afghan leadership. This doesn't mean that I never took them outside of the wire in Afghanistan; it just means that I tried to minimize their exposure to the more dangerous areas because they were not there for combat missions but rather supply, communications or personnel folks.

Fekete: Are there any similarities between combat and the legislature? If so, can you speak to that?

Ojeda: Make no mistakes about it, tactics are used in both combat and politics. In bipartisanship politics, you need to use tactics. You have to figure out how you can find common ground that both sides benefit. Sadly, when one side holds a super majority, the other side doesn't have many opportunities. During my first session I was successful in making West Virginia the 29th state to become legal for medical cannabis. I knew I did not have a snowball's chance in hell at convincing republicans to agree with me, but I chose to use the microphone to highlight the positives and call out the other legislators that chose to side with Big Pharma. Once I started giving speeches and then uploading them to social media, the community got involved.

I had requested those on social media to help me convince their legislators to support and pass my bill. In the end, we won and my bill was signed into law because if you have something that you know can benefit both sides, the people can convince those normally against it to agree for fear their constituents will remember their opposition to the bill in the next election.

Fekete: When you are leading troops, what is your self-talk like? Is there self-talk? How do you keep fatigue and fear from taking over when there is a task at hand?

Ojeda: A leader's mind never sits idle; that's proper training. Never allow yourself one course of action, have multiple. Require your subordinates to never approach you with a problem without also giving multiple courses of action to solve the problem. As far as "self-talk," whenever you are on a mission, you should have already thought through everything prior to moving out. You should already know hot spots, locations of previous attacks, you should have received intelligence briefings and ensured that all subordinates are also aware of anything that could happen during the operation. In the military the saying goes, "If you fail to plan, then you can plan to fail." This is especially true in combat. You must rehearse, rehearse, rehearse.

Fekete: Through your time in the legislature, what did you learn about government, specifically the West Virginia political landscape? About yourself? About the public in West Virginia?

Ojeda: I was honestly disappointed when I realized how little legislators want to work together for the good of the people. To realize that people care more about campaign contributions than they do their constituents. I watched people who claim to be for the people pushing legislation that killed the wage bond or removed safety on the job. I also learned that you don't have to be smart to be a legislator. Sadly, in some cases the election becomes nothing more than a popularity poll and when this happens, the people usually lose. Not everyone wants to be a politician to help. Corruption is a real problem. Even on the national scale, we are watching leaders who are caught up in insider trading. Sadly, in WV we are constantly watching our citizens vote against their own interests. This state will support sending Republican congressional candidates to Washington knowing they are in the minority and will have little opportunity to bring resources back to our state. Sadly, Trumpismis real in West Virginia. I don't know if these people will ever realize how bad that man truly was.

Fekete: Would you ever encourage your children to run for office if they expressed an interest? Why or why not?

Ojeda: Absolutely if they are passionate about something. My children watched me fight daily with other legislators. They know how tough things can be, but I am also blessed with children that research issues and stay involved with news on the national level. I have raised my children to never walk past something they know is wrong and fail to comment on it. If they do, I have told them that they will have accepted a new lower standard. As military brats, they grew up knowing that we had to make ourselves live to higher standards. In the military my spouse was a leader herself in the Family Readiness group. My kids knew that they too, were under the eyes of others. I am very pleased with my kids who are now adults that not only vote but get involved in the process.

Fekete: Who inspires you the most in your life? How?

Ojeda: This is a tough one. My father is someone that I look up to and still want to impress daily. My mother was glue that held our family together. Our grandfather was the main reason why our family has always remained strong and supportive of one another. Being made to show up every Sunday to visit with the entire family was never a chore to us. We loved it! I also served under amazing leaders in combat that to this day, I still communicate with. Those were leaders that could have spent the entire time in combat on the bases and staying safe but in the world of combat arms, mt leaders went out on the missions with the rest of us to show the troops that they too were willing to face the same hazards as we did daily. There is a lot of respect when we watched Full Bird Colonels going out with us to see the troops on the battlefield.

Fekete: Have you maintained your faith in our government? Are you jaded? Why or why not?

Ojeda: I'm jaded! It seems like we always have to settle for the lesser of two evils. In Trump's case we have had to endure the worst for the past four years, but I don't think there is a such thing as a perfect candidate. President Elect Joe Biden is far better than Donald Trump but there are still things about him that I have questions about. He's for Fracking and I think that we need to start focusing more on protecting our environment and using its natural resources like wind and solar to solve our issues. I enjoy living in a free country but after the last four years I fear we are always one election away from a dictatorship. If Donald Trump would have won this race and given four more years, I fear he would have figured out how to never step down. What's worse is that he had an entire party that was willing to allow him to do just that. I thought we have finally elevated ourselves after two successful presidential races with President Barrack Hussein Obama but Donald Trump has succeeded in making this nation hate again and I realize we are nowhere near eradicating racism. He proved its alive and well in 2020.

Fekete: West Virginia is famous for its worker's rights history and you hail from a coal mining family. How did this shape who you are today? Do you believe this gives you an edge? Does it hold you back in any way?

Ojeda: You and I grew up in a family that was rich in coal mining. Our grandfather laid track in the mines into his seventies. My other grandfather was killed in a coal mining collapse. Watching strikes when we were younger showed us the importance of standing up for yourself, even if you were outnumbered. I remember watching coal trucks push cars off of a bridge at the entrance of Dehue. I remember watching a video of our uncle Kippy being arrested during a strike that got violent. Growing up, the UMWA played a vital role in our family. Every miner was also a member of the UMWA. Years later I would receive their endorsement when I ran for congress and that meant the world to me. Sadly, I would later find out that they are just like any other political operation that behind the scenes, makes deals that are just as underhanded as any other group that uses politics and plays both sides to get what they want. I think if the dues paying members really knew what went on behind the scenes, many would stop paying dues immediately.

Fekete: Can you tell us what you've been up to lately? What's your focus now?

Ojeda: I am now the national spokesman for No Dem Left Behind that focuses on flipping red seats blue in rural America. Currently we are working with other organizations to focus on the two senate runoff races in Georgia to try and flip the senate blue and send Mitch McConnel to the back of the room.

Fekete: I heard you're starting a podcast and Andrew Yang is your first guest. What inspired you to start podcasting? What can you tell us about the podcast, its purpose, intended audience, and what we can expect to hear?

Ojeda: The podcast will be called "Airborne" and I will be the host. Andrew Yang and others will be on the show and we will focus on current operations and plans for the future. We are not just bringing on the easy interviews where we all get along but we are also looking at controversial folks that we think need to be questioned about past practices.

Fekete: Sometimes when we choose a specific path, we end up on another. What path are you on now? Where have you been and where are you going?

Ojeda: I have been blessed to travel the world. I am currently focusing on relocating my entire family and continuing with No Dem Left Behind. I am currently planning a 40-day trip to Europe where I may also be speaking at Oxford University. I was blessed last year to do the same thing at Yale University. I still find it funny that people want to hear my opinions, but I enjoy speaking about politics, my experiences and my plans. If what I say can inspire someone to challenge themselves then I have done my job.

Fekete: Can you speak ideas such as faith, fate, and purpose? What do you believe in now?

Ojeda: I am not a very religious person. It's not that I do not believe in God. I jumped out of airplanes for 20 years and lived in combat zones for multiple years. I was almost killed 5 times in Iraq and captured in Afghanistan. I believe I survived those experiences because God has other plans for me. I survived a brutal attack that was supposed to kill me after I had retired and was running for state senate. I no longer follow any church because I think in most cases it's a racket just to fleece the flock. I have now decided that I will try to do good things for good people. When I do, it makes me feel good. I'm going to stick with that. You don't need to tithe to a mad behind a pulpit. Buy a coat for a man who is homeless. Pay for the meal when you know the person behind you at the drive through is a struggling single mother with children.

Fekete: What's next for you? You're working with a ghostwriter on an autobiography. What do you hope to accomplish by telling your story?

Ojeda: I am currently working on a book that focuses on occupations and groups of people who have been forgotten. The elderly, the addicted, Unions etc. We allow our first responders and teachers to struggle in society today when they are absolutely some of the most important people we have in society. The book focuses on ways we can do better and also dabbles in how a Universal Basic Income could be the difference between an elderly person making it from month to month without having to dumpster dive. Sadly, that exists today. But I thought we were the greatest nation on earth?

Fekete: You really inspire people who hear you speak. What words do you have now for the people who supported you and wished you'd have stayed in politics?

Ojeda: Keep following me. I'm not done. I'm not running in West Virginia ever again, but I will always be a voice for those that don't have the ability to speak up. I'm retired US Army, and I have secured residual income to where I can say what I want, and I don't have to worry about losing everything. That's why they tried to kill me. I wasn't scared to lose my job when I took on a thirty-six-year politician that ran our county with an iron fist. He usually ran unopposed because people feared him. I didn't....and I won.

BIO

Over the past 24 years Richard Ojeda has served in Europe and Korea with deployments to Honduras, Chile and Jordan. He is a Cold War Veteran and has deployed three times (two combat) in support of Operation Iraqi Freedom and once to Afghanistan for Operation Enduring Freedom. He served during the humanitarian mission to Haiti immediately following the 2010 earthquake. He holds a BA from West Virginia State University and an MA from Webster University. He is a graduate of both, the Basic and Advanced Engineer Officer Courses as well as the Command General Staff College. Awards and decorations include: Two Bronze Star Medals, the Sapper Tab, The Master Parachutist Badge. Air Assault Badge, The Combat Action Badge. The Engineer Bronze Order of the De Fleury Medal. He is the 47th member in the 20th Engineer Brigades history to achieve the status of Centurion Jumper. Major Ojeda holds parachutist badges from seven foreign countries as well as a German Marksmanship award. He is the first American selected to attend the Chilean Commando Scuba Course. Pending the Purple Heart. He was selected for promotion to the rank of Lieutenant Colonel, but retired to relocate to Logan County, West Virginia where he co-founded the LEAD Community Organization and worked to establish a JROTC program in the schools across Logan. LEAD has sent over 6000 students to school with new shoes, served over 10,000 meals to the elderly, homeless, and sick and has responded to countless disasters from floods to fires. In 2016 he became WV state senator (7th District) and in his first session, Currently Richard Ojeda is the National Spokesman for No Dem Left Behind helping candidates in rural, red districts flip red seats blue. He is married to Kelly Ojeda. They have two children, Kayla and Richard III.

Interview with Chet Lowther on His New Book "Trumpty Dumpty and the Great Wall"

Available now online and in major bookstores. Published by Guest Room Press/Black Crown Books.

An anonymous reviewer says of the book: "This book is about a great wall, a fabulous wall, a much better wall than the one in Jina, built by the Greatest Wall Builder in history, a stable genius, this guy. He knows more about walls than anybody. I didn't read it past the cover, too many words, but I'm sure it ends well. These things always do. It's fabulous. It's a fabulous book. It's going to be huge. Five stars!"

Question: How did the character of Trumpty Dumpty first come about in your work?

Chet I started Trumpty shortly after the last election. It was probably some sort of coping mechanism. I was in disbelief that we had elected such a character as President. Trump provides lots of inspiration for satire.

Q: What medium do you most often work with? What did you use for Trumpty?

Chet I work with a variety of mediums, en caustic, oil, acrylic, sculpture, etc. I started Trumpty with gouache, but ended up using liquid acrylic and pen

Q: You're a visual artist, not an author, so how did this evolved into a book?

Chet: I am not an author, but I am a songwriter. Once I got the idea, the verse and images poured out, which often happens in the songwriting process.

Q: When did you know you wanted to paint Trump?

Chet: My first painting of Trump was during the 2016 campaign, a huge portrait for a black-light show at a local gallery. It was my first and last black-light painting. Then, they had a propaganda-themed show at that same gallery, so I painted Trump as "Uncle Sham."

Q: Do you often paint political figures? I know you have some work of the infamous coal baron Don Blankenship. Why paint Don?

Chet: I hadn't done much political work since the Bush administration, way back when I mistakenly thought things couldn't get any worse. I carved a series of caricature pumpkins dubbed the "Repumplicans." Don Blankenship was the first in a series that I planned using dollar signs in a pointillist style, the series was going to be called "Portraits of American Greed." I soon realized I would never run out of material.

Q: Are there any connections or parallels in your mind between those two figures? Don Blankenship and Donald Trump?

Chet: Both men put profit over people and represent the darkest side of Corporate America.

Q: What made you want to seek publication for Trumpty Dumpty?

Chet: I think there could be a market for it.

Q: What is it like seeing the final product of your work?

Chet: It feels really good to see the final product. I have a real sense of relief that I finally finished it.

Q: Do you think these sorts of satirical books play an important role in public discourse surrounding elections?

Chet: I think satire is important, if we couldn't laugh once in a while we would constantly be cursing or crying.

Q: Your book is very critical of the administration as a whole, how do you feel about Trump or his fans seeing it?

Chet: I hope Trump sees it, a tweet about it would be great publicity. Hopefully his fans might have a sense of humor. I mean, they worship a cartoon character, so they must.

Q: Do you think you'll write another book?

Chet: I don't have plans to write another book. I sure hope I don't need to write a sequel unless it's called, "Trumpty...... from the White House to the Big House." I wouldn't mind writing that one.

Pictured: The Editor. Andréa Fekete. Circa 2000. Photo Credit: Cooter Rasputin. Fekete is curently lone editor and designer of this journal. She has mostly left the social media matrix, so to speak with her you have to actually pick up the phone like back in the day when people didn't have social media. She made this journal because she believes in art, her friends, and enjoys making new friends who make art. She's a published novelist, poet, and co-editor of one award-winning anthology of women's writing, *Feminine Rising: Voices of Power and Invisibility.* She's sometimes an adjunct professor of writing and literature. She holds a BA and MA in English and MFA in writing courtesy of Marshall University and WV Wesleyan College. She sometimes helps people publish or edit their own work. As you can see from this photo, she used to smoke cigarettes. She still stands around talking writing with her friends, but no longer smokes because now she knows better. For some reason she still writes even though she knows better. She thinks she's hilarious and most days believes she writes things that are mostly not terrible (now that she's done it for 30 years). This is only Fekete's 2nd time using Adobe Indesign, so she's stoked the magazine is legible. (can you read this?) Fekete's poetry and fiction appear in many journals and anthologies such as *Chiron Review, Borderlands: Texas Poetry Review, The Kentucky Review, The Adirondack Review, ABZ,* and in anthologies such as E*yes Glowing at the Edge of the Woods: Fiction & Poetry from West Virginia* among many others. This may or may not be the last issue of this journal. If there is another, it will also probably be the last. Read reviews of her work and learn more about her at hollergirl.com

Taryn Conn, featured photographer

Taryn Conn was born and raised in the beautiful Appalachian mountains in Buffalo Creek, WV. She is head trail manager for the Hatfield-McCoy Trail Systems, the largest ATV trail system on the East coast. She spends each day in the woods leading a team that cares for those hundreds of miles of trials, where she often finds inspiration for her photos. She began taking photos during her time in the hills as a teenager. Over a decade later, she is still learning to play with light and dark, birth and decay. Her work has appeared at such venues as Blank Gallery and West Edge Factory in Huntington, WV, and has been featured in such literary journals as *Pine, Mountain, Sand and Gravel*.

CPSIA information can be obtained
at www.ICGtesting.com
Printed in the USA
BVHW021203250521
608002BV00011BA/2124